Tevye's Daughters: No Laughing Matter

The Women behind the Story of *Fiddler on the Roof*

OTHER BOOKS BY JAN LISA HUTTNER

PENNY'S PICKS:
50 MOVIES BY WOMEN FILMMAKERS

DIAMOND FIDDLER:
LADEN WITH HAPPINESS & TEARS
THE STORIES BEHIND THE STORY OF **FIDDLER** ON **THE ROOF**

Tevye's Daughters

No Laughing Matter

The Women behind the Story of Fiddler on the Roof

By Jan Lisa Huttner

First Edition 2014
ISBN 978-0-9850964-4-1
© FF2 Media (2014)
Graphic design by Melissa Wilks

Second Edition 2018
ISBN 978-0-9850964-5-8
© FF2 Media LLC (2018)
Design Consultant: Allison Nordin

FF2 Media® LLC logo design by Jan Lisa Huttner & Ray Marrero (2016)
Little fiddler on the spine by Karen Wegehenkel (2016)

This book is dedicated to:

Chaya Esther Rabinowitz

Rachel Yampolsky

Olga Loyeff

Marie Waife-Goldberg

Without these four women—his mother, his mother-in-law, his wife, and his youngest daughter—the name "Sholem Aleichem" would not have the worldwide resonance it has today.

May their memories be for blessing.

TABLE OF CONTENTS

PHOTOS & ILLUSTRATIONS

© Richard Bayard Miller (2012)

The Jerome Robbins Centennial Edition

"Why is the sky blue? Why? Why? Why?"

Young children ask a lot of questions, so I am sure I asked my share. But the first question I actually remember asking is this one: Daddy, if both of these books are about Joan of Arc, then why are they different inside?

My father loved books about history and current events, and by third grade I had already learned that reading was a sure way to get his attention. So I combed the library shelves in the children's section for biographies about famous people, and weekly book reports became part of our regular Sunday routine.

One day, I found two books about Joan of Arc. I must have been intrigued by this phenomenon because I took both of them down from the shelf and added them to my pile. To my surprise, the differences between these two books did not stop at their covers; the words inside were different too.

To say that I remember actual details about this momentous event in my life would be a lie. But the impact of this tiny incident—some sixty years ago—defies the passage of time. I know I showed my father two books about Joan of Arc. I know I was confused because, even though they were about the same person, they were different. I know I asked him why.

Why were the contents of the two books different? "Because even though the subject is the same, the two books were written

1

by different people, and each writer sees things his own way." My father must have said something like this, and his response was my introduction to what I would one day learn to call "epistemology" (the study of knowledge). Without any familiarity whatsoever with Jean Piaget and the Three Mountain Task, my father had just taught me the psychological principle of "decentration."

But looking back all these years later, does it really matter what my father actually said? I think what matters most is that he took my question seriously, thereby encouraging me to keep asking questions. And for that reason, I can see my father's smile on every page of this little book.

In "The Great Windfall" (the first story that Sholem Aleichem ever wrote about Tevye-the-Dairyman), Tevye says he has seven daughters. But in *Fiddler on the Roof*, the Broadway musical based on Sholem Aleichem's eight Tevye stories, Tevye tells the audience several times—without any explanation or qualification—that he has five daughters: "I have five daughters."

Eddie Huttner's daughter wanted to know why. If there are seven daughters in the Tevye stories, then why are there only five daughters in *Fiddler on the Roof*? The question gnawed at me and it would not let me rest.

I was in third grade in 1959; ten years later, I was a college student. On my first Friday night at St. John's College in Annapolis, Maryland, our new dean—Robert A. Goldwin—gave a lecture called "St. John's College Asks John Locke Some Questions." At the beginning of his lecture, Dean Goldwin made the following assertion. "Asked with good timing… the perceptive 'Why?' can transform your thinking and lead you into entirely new paths."

But then Dean Goldwin injected a note of caution. Before becoming obsessed with a "Why?" question, Dean Goldwin recommended that we ask a "simple, earthy, challenging, impertinent question: 'So what?'"

> To say, "So what?" is not the same as to say, "Who cares?" "Who cares?" is a non-question because it expresses a lack of wonder, a lack of concern, a disinclination to inquiry…
>
> On the other hand, to ask, "So what?" means to ask, "tell me why I should care… "
>
> I am certain that Locke wanted you to ask him probing and impertinent questions. I am certain that he hoped to attract just such questioning readers… He wanted readers who would say as they read, "You say the state of nature, Mr. Locke, and I say 'So what?'" (Goldwin, Page 1)

This simple distinction between "So What?" and "Who Cares?" also made an enormous impression on me, and in the five decades since I first heard Dean Goldwin's lecture in 1969, I have always tried to bring a "So What?" mindset to each new problem before allowing myself to indulge in the shrug of a "Who Cares?" Luckily, in this second instance, I actually have a paper trail!

I began my research on *Fiddler on the Roof* the way most people do, by reading Sholem Aleichem. The eight Tevye stories were published one-by-one over a span of almost twenty years, but are now typically read together as a "novel in real time" called *Tevye the Dairyman*. Having grown up with the voice of Zero Mostel as Tevye braying "I have five daughters!" at the very beginning of the *Fiddler on the Roof* Original Cast Album, I was quite surprised to learn, in the very first of the eight Tevye stories, that Sholem Aleichem had actually given Tevye seven daughters. But, to be quite honest, it took several years of research on other aspects of *Fiddler on the Roof* before the exact number of daughters became an urgent question for me.

My implicit "Who cares?" stance—reflecting my "lack of wonder, lack of concern, disinclination to inquiry"—suddenly flipped overnight. The timing was finally right, and just as Dean Goldwin had predicted, this "Why?" question transformed my thinking. The search for an answer led me "into entirely new paths" and each new thing I learned pushed me ever deeper until I finally found the surprising source hiding right in plain sight in—of all places—the Bible.

After I published this book in September 2014, I received many "So What?" responses that often turned into a gratifying "Who Knew?" once the reader had actually read my book. But I also received a lot of "Who Cares?" shrugs when I tried to interest people in a new take on an old topic.

To be clear, I am not saying everyone needs to care. I fully appreciate that most people are already very busy living their lives. So although I have tried my best to be as intriguing as I believe this particular subject—*Fiddler on the Roof*—deserves, I may well have lost you as a reader forever. If so, then may The Force be with you!

But some people should care, especially people who are interested in stories about women, and people who typically subordinate stories about women to stories about men. For better or for worse, many women fall into category one and all too many men fall into category two. So let me be very clear:

- If you think you already know Sholem Aleichem, then you should care about the contents of this book.

- If you think *Fiddler on the Roof* is about Tevye, then you should care about the contents of this book.

- If you love Jane Austen, then you should care about the contents of this book.

- If you are a *Downton Abbey* fan, then you should care about the contents of this book.

- If you care about the women in the Bible, then you should definitely care about the contents of this book.

"So What?" is a deliberately rude and impertinent question, but after years of research, I am ready for it. And if you read this book, then I know you will find answers that will surprise you. But if you read this book and all you are left with at the end is "Who Cares?" then the obvious answer is "Not You."

Questions can be dangerous and if you push hard enough, you will often find yourself contesting Conventional Wisdom. In this case, just because Tevye says he has seven daughters in "The Great Windfall" (the first story that Sholem Aleichem ever wrote about Tevye-the-Dairyman), does that mean Tevye actually has seven daughters in *Tevye the Dairyman* (the "novel in real time" which contains the eight Tevye stories)?

I know it sounds preposterous, but this is one of the reasons some people think the creators of *Fiddler on the Roof* were somehow dismissive of Sholem Aleichem, demeaning his greatest work with their adaptation rather than honoring it. "Sholem Aleichem gave Tevye seven daughters, but you only gave him five!"

Read *Tevye the Dairyman* for yourself, however, and by the end you will realize that despite what is said in the first story, Sholem Aleichem himself only gave Tevye five daughters (by which I mean he only wrote stories about five daughters). When Tevye leaves his home at the end of "Get Thee Out" (the final story), readers know what has become of the five daughters named in *Fiddler on the Roof*—Tzeitel, Hodel, Chava, Shprintze, and Bielke—even if their trajectories are not quite the same. But somewhere along the way, two daughters vanished. Therefore, it is

5

Sholem Aleichem himself, not the creators of *Fiddler on the Roof*, who has disappeared them. So much for Conventional Wisdom.

To me, the most amazing revelation about this rabbit hole I have fallen down is that it still has no bottom. Although I have now spent over fifteen years of my life doing serious analytical research on *Fiddler on the Roof*, huge questions remain unanswered. My biggest question is this: What did Joseph Stein know and when did he know it?

Stein, the author of *Fiddler on the Roof*'s "book" (the theatrical term for the "libretto" in an opera), had limited access to many of the resources that have become critical to me in my own research, most especially *My Father, Sholom Aleichem* (the biography Marie Waife-Goldberg published about her famous father in 1968), and Sholem Aleichem's autobiography *From the Fair* (published in Yiddish in 1916, but not released in a full English translation until 1985).

So how was Stein able to zero in with such acute specificity on incidents alluded to in texts that had not yet been published?

On the other hand, one question that I had left open in 2014 is now closed. Did Sholem Aleichem know about the five Daughters of Zelophehad, women who are individuated three times by name in the Book of Numbers? The answer is yes. Yes, Sholem Aleichem definitely knew what the Lord had commanded in the matter of the five named daughters of Zelophehad. He knew all about how Rashi had praised them as well.

I discovered this unequivocal answer quite inadvertently while I was working on edits to *Diamond Fiddler: Laden with Happiness & Tears*. The whole story is now there (in the section called "Why Not King Lear?"), so I will not repeat it here. Suffice it to say that on page 231 of Curt Leviant's 1985 translation of Sholem Aleichem's autobiography *From the Fair*, Sholem Aleichem talks about the day he met Elimelech Loyev (his future father-in-law) for the first time.

"Listen here, young fellow, let me ask you something," old Loyev sang out. "My son [Joshua]
tells me that you're just as knowledgeable in our
holy Jewish books as in their secular ones. Do
you remember what Rashi says about the daughters of Zelophehad?" (Leviant, Page 232)

I had read these words when I first read Curt Leviant's translation of *From the Fair* (which was probably in 2011), but they had
not registered. Since I had yet to appreciate the full significance of
the story of the Daughters of Zelophehad, this reference to them in
Sholem Aleichem's autobiography had gone right over my head…

But then, I had a new question: Was this "memory" true?
After all these years of research, I have learned to be extremely
cautious about memories (including my own), so I honestly had
no idea. However, this Robbins Centennial Edition includes a
new appendix in which I argue for the affirmative. Just as I look
back on my own life now and find myself discussing Joan of Arc
with my father, Sholem Aleichem looked back on his life and
found himself discussing the Daughters of Zelophehad with his
future father-in-law.

So speaking personally—for myself—I do feel that the last
pieces of this particular puzzle have finally fallen into place… I
may never be able to prove it, but my heart tells me this is how it
happened. Solomon Rabinowitz (aka Sholem Aleichem) did indeed embed the story of the Daughters of Zelophehad in the text
of *Tevye the Dairyman*.

While he may well have started out with a Yiddish proverb
about the father of seven daughters, by the time he wrote the
eighth and final Tevye story "Get Thee Out!", the number five—
for five daughters—had taken on deep symbolic significance
for him not just personally and artistically, but spiritually too.
("Adonai: Why did I have to live my life worrying about five dowries?") Why do I think these dowries continued to plague him?
Because he specifically mentions dowries for his first two grand-

daughters—the only grandchildren he lived to see—in his famous ethical will.

> And as to my works in Hebrew, they belong to their masterful translator, my son-in-law, I.D. Berkovits, and to his daughter, my grandchild, Tamar (Tamara) Berkovits—that should be her dowry. Of the royalties that might arrive for my plays both in Russia and America, half should go to my family and half should be put away in the name of granddaughter Bella, the daughter of Mikhoel and Sarah Kaufman—let that be her dowry. (Zuckerman & Herbst, Page 483)

And all of these daughters, had any of them ever read *Pride and Prejudice*? My heart tells me, once again, that the answer is yes. Yes, the daughters of Solomon and Olga Rabinowitz, and their mother, and their father's ward Natasha, had all read *Pride and Prejudice*. And the author Sholem Aleichem knew about the five Bennet daughters in *Pride and Prejudice* because that is the kind of home in which a real man named Solomon Rabinowitz wrote *Tevye the Dairyman*.

And what did Joseph Stein know and when did he know it? Well, whatever he knew, *Fiddler on the Roof* is "a perfect fit, made to measure."

The questions in this little book are incessant. And yet one of the things I have learned by falling down this rabbit hole, is that this cry "Why? Why?? Why???" has been the cry of my people— the Jewish people—from the beginning.

In my sophomore year at St. John's College, I began attending a weekly Torah Study class taught by Simon Kaplan. Mr. Kaplan, a courtly gentleman educated in Europe who was an Emeritus Tutor in those years, always began each new year with a question I will never forget. "Why does the Bible begin with the letter Bet in the word Bereshit?"

After allowing his students some time to speculate, his definitive answer was something like this: "You must not look up or down, or worry about what might have come before 'the beginning.' Just keep reading the words of the text." Mr. Kaplan, who died on March 13, 1979, was also a Kant scholar. When I took his preceptorial on the *Critique of Pure Reason* in my senior year, he tried to soothe my anxiety with these unforgettable words: "Space and Time? It's not so difficult, Miss Huttner. Side-by-Side and One-after-Another." It was the same basic message I had always received from my father: "No matter what happens, Jan, you just keep on keepin' on."

My people—the Jewish people—do this every year, year after year. Once the High Holidays are over, we go back to Parsha Bereshit (the first Torah portion) and we start reading the words of the text all over again. And wonder of wonders, miracle of miracles, year after year, we always hear something anew or see something anew, so we start asking questions about something, something that was always there, but has suddenly taken on fresh meaning. If there is one "tradition," more than any other, that defines *us* as a people, this is it.

But in the interim, something terrible has happened: Jewish men have risen up in force to tell Jewish women we must not use our voices in public, especially in the synagogue. We should stay silent—preferably behind a barrier called a "mechitzah"—lest we disturb them or "distract" them while they are praying. In some Orthodox neighborhoods now, women must walk on one side of the street while men walk on the other. If women board a bus, they must move to the back.

And as extremists often do, they have sent their poison into the world, far beyond the Jewish community. By invoking the principle of "modesty," some Jewish newspapers in the United

States went so far as to disappear Hillary Rodham Clinton—who was America's Secretary of State at the time—from photos of the Situation Room in the White House on the day Osama Bin Laden was finally captured and executed.

Because of my devotion to all things *Fiddler*, I now know better and I will not be intimidated. I know that in Parsha B'Shallah in the Book of Exodus:

> Miriam the prophetess took a timbrel in her hand, and all the women went out with her in dance with timbrels. And Miriam **chanted** for them: "Sing to the Lord…" Exodus 15:20–21 (Etz Hayim, Page 412)

I know that in the notes on page 412, this section is actually called "The **Song** of Miriam," and the comments on it are as follows:

> These verses [vv.20–1] affirm the custom (chronicled in Judg. 11:34 and 1 Sam. 18:6) of women going forth with music and dance to hail a returning victorious hero, although God and not man is the victor.

I know that in our prayer book, the *Mishkan HaNefesh*, this moment is celebrated in one of Judaism's most joyous songs:

> Mi-chamocha ba-eilim, Adonai? Of all that is worshiped, is there another like You? (Page 164)

I know that the words that precede the actual song itself are:

> **Sing** praise to God Most High, most blessed source of blessing, as Moses, Miriam, and **all** Israel sang this joyous song to You… (Page 162)

And I even know that the Haftorah for this parsha, taken from the Book of Judges (Etz Hayim, Page 427), is called "The **Song** of Deborah and Barak" and includes the line:

> On that day Deborah and Barak son of Abinoam **sang**: "I will sing, will sing to the Lord…"

© Horne and Brewer (1908)

So who are these men who are so adamant in the 21st century (the 21st century!), these men who bully us and tell us—me and all my Jewish sisters—that "modesty" requires us to silence ourselves, rarely speaking in public, much less singing?

Don't they know that Miriam sang and Deborah sang?

Don't they know that Moses, Miriam, and all Israel sang this joyous song now known as "Mi-chamocha" at the Sea of Reeds?

Don't they know that Mahlah, No'ah, Hoglah, Milcah, and Tirzah (the Five Daughters of Zelophehad):

> ...stood before Moses, Eleazar the priest, the chieftains, and the whole assembly, at the entrance of the Tent of Meeting, and they said, "Let not our father's name be lost to his clan just because he had no son! Give us a holding among our father's kinsmen!" (Etz Hayim, Page 926)

Don't they know that:

> Moses brought their case before the Lord. And the Lord said to Moses, "The plea of Zelophehad's daughters is just: you should give them a hereditary holding among their father's kinsmen; transfer their father's share to them." (Etz Hayim, Page 927)

If they do not know these things, then they are not reading their Torah, much less studying it. If they do not know these things, then they have deliberately disappeared the words of Judaism's core text. If they do not know these things, then it is because they do not want to. Well, maybe they don't, but I do.

Obsessed by all things *Fiddler*, I needed to know more about Jewish "tradition," so I began attending Services on a regular basis. Now my mind is filled with the words of wonderful Rabbis—Rabbi Batsheva Appel (at KAM Isaiah Israel in Chicago), Rabbi Carie Carter (at Park Slope Jewish Center in Brooklyn), and Rabbi Heidi Hoover (at Temple Beth Emeth in Brooklyn)—who have stood before my congregations and led Services. And now my heart is filled with the music of wonderful Cantors and Cantorial Soloists—Miriam Ashkenazi, Suzanne Bernstein, Leslie Newcorn, Judy Ribnick, and Nonie Schuster Donato—who have led my congregations in songs and prayers. Adonai has blessed the voices of all of these women who stand so proudly on the bemah, and only Adonai will ever silence them. Only Adonai can ever silence me.

This book—*Tevye's Daughters: No Laughing Matter*—was published in 2014 in honor of the 50th anniversary of the first

Broadway performance of *Fiddler on the Roof*. I published another book—*Diamond Fiddler: Laden with Happiness & Tears*—in 2016 in honor of Sholem Aleichem's 100th Yahrzeit. I think of this first book, which only pursues the significance of the number five in "I have five daughters," as an appetizer course, a literary amuse-bouche. *Diamond Fiddler*, on the other hand, is a much more comprehensive attack on the Conventional Wisdom that has weighed *Fiddler on the Roof* down for over 50 years. *Diamond Fiddler* is a meal.

Now, in 2018, I am reissuing both books in honor of the Jerome Robbins Centennial with new covers, new graphics, and indexes which should make it easier for readers to find the topics which are of most interest to them personally. Also, typos and other minor errors have been reduced thanks to the sharp eyes of several editors and many friends. I am particularly grateful to Yosani Brewer, Katherine Factor, Brigid Presecky, and Pilar Wyman, for their invaluable assistance through many ups and downs.

It also took two attorneys—Judith Grubner in Chicago and Richard Jacobson in New York—to resolve an inadvertent copyright issue. I thank them both for seeing the matter through to its successful conclusion. Sharon Rosenzweig has designed the cover for this new edition. If you like it, you will love her contributions to *Diamond Fiddler*. Dorthea Juul has been a faithful friend, and Alicia Garvey has been my guardian angel.

To my husband, Richard Bayard Miller, wherever we are, "There with my love, I'm home." Now, let us begin!

Jan Lisa Huttner
Brooklyn, NY
October 11, 2018

© Sally Heckel (2008)

Prologue:
The "Me Search" in the Research

Date: Saturday, May 20, 2000
Time: Approximately 7:00 AM
Place: A balcony on the 9th floor of Hotel Le Meridien in Nice

I had arrived in France on Thursday evening with my husband Richard and my mother-in-law Juanita. We were there to celebrate Juanita's 75th birthday. ("Why should we have a party in Florida," she'd said, "when we can use this opportunity to go somewhere else?") I was a health care computer consultant exhausted by Y2K projects, and all I wanted was a stress-free vacation. After much discussion, we picked a tour called the Riviera's Artistic Legacies.

Friday morning, we boarded a bus and headed off to our first stop: the Matisse Museum in Cimiez. Four delightful hours later, with one stop for a brief but delicious lunch, we arrived at the Marc Chagall National Biblical Message Museum. I walked through the door, and suddenly everything turned serious.

Abraham preparing Isaac for sacrifice! Jacob wrestling with the angel! Moses parting the Red Sea! And look: there's Jesus on the cross—wearing a tallis as a loincloth!

I had walked in thinking I already knew everything I needed to know about Marc Chagall ("kitsch," nu?), but I fell headlong into these huge, dynamic canvases. There is a name for what happened to me that day; scholars call it "aesthetic arrest."

When our guide started herding us back to the bus, I ran into the gift shop and quickly purchased one of the English picture books: *Marc Chagall* by Andrew Kagan.

Back on the bus, I listened quietly as folks around me discussed the day. Such vibrant colors! Such wonderful food! But nothing I heard matched the buzz in my head. That's when I suddenly realized that I was the only Jew in our group. Like most Jewish Americans, I live in a world filled with Christian iconography, but I knew I was seeing, *really seeing*, "biblical messages" from the brush of a Jewish artist for the very first time in my life, and Chagall's imagery had pierced something deep in my soul. I kept my thoughts to myself. This was no time to discuss weighty matters. We were in a rush. We had dinner reservations at the Hotel Negresco!

The next morning I got up early, ordered breakfast, and took a quick shower. When the room service waiter arrived, I steered him quietly past my sleeping husband and onto the balcony, and after he left, I poured myself a cup of coffee and began reading. Chagall's *The Green Musician* actually appears opposite the title page in this particular book, but I flipped right past him. I read and read with growing fascination until I reached page 48:

> In the allegory of music, a theme Chagall
> repeated in the animated *The Green Musician*,
> appears once again his fiddler on the roof, that
> stock character preserved from the world of the
> shtetl by Chagall and Sholem Aleichem.

I turned back and looked at the image of *The Green Musician* (officially titled *Green Violinist* according to the Guggenheim). "Oh, my God," I said out loud. "It's THE fiddler on the roof!"

Chagall's "fiddler on the roof"—we all know him, right? Of course, right! He appears regularly on book jackets, catalogs and coloring books, CD and DVD covers, note cards, art stickers, and all kinds of tchotchkes… But how well do we really know him?

Fiddler on the Roof had always been "there" in the background of my life, so much so that I can't even tell you when or how any of it first embedded itself in my consciousness; all I can say for sure is that it was never prominent in any way. The Broadway embodiment of Sholem Aleichem's characters and Marc Chagall's images was simply a part of my cultural heritage, and since I was a serious-minded young lady with high intellectual aspirations, I barely gave it a second thought.

I was born in 1951, and I grew up in northern New Jersey, so I am sure I saw *Fiddler on the Roof* on Broadway, but I have no memory of it. (On the other hand, I have vivid memories of the day my mother took me into Manhattan to see *Man of La Mancha* in 1965.) I am also certain that I saw the film version of *Fiddler on the Roof* when it was released in 1971, but I have no memory of that either. (On the other hand, I can provide specific details about the first time I saw *Funny Girl* in 1969.) It's quite likely that I saw Chagall's *The Green Musician* at the Guggenheim Museum—the painting they call *Green Violinist* in their online collection—but all I remember now is the dramatic staircase. (On the other hand, I can picture a teenage me at New York's Museum of Modern Art standing in awe before Picasso's *Guernica*.) There is only one thing about my early encounters with *Fiddler on the Roof* that I can say with absolute certainty: we owned a copy of the Original Broadway Cast Album. After my father died, I took that well-worn LP home with me; it is sitting right now on a shelf in my office.

But I have just described the exact moment—on May 20, 2000—that I became obsessed with all things *Fiddler*. Something I had always taken for granted suddenly became the focal point of deep mysteries, and my life turned inside out. Scholars have a name for that too; they call it a "paradigm shift."

We flew home on Sunday, May 28. The next day was Memorial Day, and the day after that I went back to work. When I told people that the trip to France had "changed my life," they were ready to listen, but I was tongue-tied. Even my husband, who certainly knew "something" had happened, wouldn't have been able to tell you what—although he certainly knew I was suddenly buying a lot of old books on Amazon—books about Marc Chagall, books by Sholem Aleichem, and books on the history of Broadway.

I learned on the internet that other people also wondered why the popular musical about Tevye and his family was called *Fiddler on the Roof*. Was the title connected to the Chagall painting and, if so, what was the significance of the connection? Mysteries multiplied; every new thing I learned raised a new set of questions.

On Tuesday morning, September 4, 2001, I quit my consulting job. Lots of little things had happened in my life between May 20, 2000 and September 4, 2001, and something very big happened to all of us exactly one week later on September 11, 2001. So I am not saying that I quit my job just to devote myself to *Fiddler on the Roof*, but clearly the fact that fourteen years later I am still obsessed with all things *Fiddler* is proof enough that my life really did change that Saturday morning in Nice.

The daily life I live now bears almost no resemblance to the daily life I lived then. I have carved out a third act for myself in the evolving world of new media. I write articles for print and online editors, I post on several websites and blogs of my own creation, and I spend way too much time on Facebook. The book which follows presents a summary of one line of *Fiddler* research pertaining to Tevye's daughters. I have much more to say on this topic, and I plan to publish a full book by May 13, 2016 (the date of Sholem Aleichem's 100th Yahrzeit). But I could not let September 22, 2014—the date of the first Broadway performance of *Fiddler on the Roof*—go by without offering my personal tribute to the creators of this great cultural achievement.

My work on *Fiddler on the Roof* has moved along two tracks which I call "Sources" and "Synergies."

Sources are deliberate references intended by, and readily acknowledged, by the creators. In this case, the creators of *Fiddler on the Roof* have been very clear about their sources. Many of the words, in the lyrics written by Sheldon Harnick as well as in the libretto written by Joseph Stein, come directly from one of eight Tevye stories written over two decades by Sholem Aleichem—eight separate stories which are typically collected and published as one "novel" called *Tevye the Dairyman*. Most of the images in the original set which Boris Aronson designed for director Jerome Robbins in 1964 echo Chagall canvases (not just the Guggenheim's *Green Violinist*, but *I and the Village* and others as well).

Synergies are more allusive and therefore more controversial. They also carry more historical weight. Something that might have been "common knowledge" at the time of creation might well be deeply buried 50 years later. When I began my research in earnest in 2002, I had a long list of people I wanted to talk to, but over time, as my interest in archival research grew, my interest in what people thought they remembered steadily decreased.

In part this was because the people I most wanted to talk to—first and foremost Jerome Robbins, Marc Chagall, Boris Aronson, and Marie Waife-Goldberg—were long gone. Also the more I searched, the more discrepancies surfaced between what people "remembered" and what I found in the archives. When push comes to shove, I will always choose original documentation over memory.

Now that I am a writer myself, I have also had opportunities to interview a great many creative people in the past decade, and most of them will readily admit that their own work is full of synergies. Allusions are not always conscious, and when I probe, these artists typically respond with warmth. One day, I asked Deborah Kampmeier, an American filmmaker, if she had intended to make deliberate references to *The Scarlet Letter* when she wrote her *Virgin* screenplay. Her reply: "I hadn't consciously thought of it, but I like it."

On another day, I asked Nir Bergman, an Israeli filmmaker, if he was consciously thinking about the assassination of Yitzhak Rabin when he wrote his *Broken Wings* screenplay. He reacted with surprise: "In the first scene that I wrote for the script, before I knew what the whole script would be about, a family lost their dog on the day that Rabin was murdered. Eventually, that scene just got dropped. The script was going different places. But that was the first scene."

How did I know? In both cases I knew—or to be more accurate, I guessed—because I shared deep common frameworks with these two filmmakers. In each case, I could feel the resonance as I watched their films.

I am a graduate of St. John's College in Annapolis, Maryland ("the Great Books School"), and at St. John's we were taught to think about the authors of the Great Books as participants in a Great Conversation. This is not "plagiarism." Educated people always find their nourishment in the creative work of others. Our hearts and our minds absorb the ideas of those who came before us just as much as our bodies absorb the protein in the eggs we eat for breakfast.

Ultimately, whenever I doubt myself—which is often—I console myself with this thought: *Hamlet* was first performed sometime between 1599 and 1602, and yet today, over 400 years later, people are still arguing about it. No one alive today can ask William Shakespeare for his input. All scholars can do is make their best case.

Do I really mean to compare *Fiddler on the Roof* with *Hamlet*? Yes, I do. I think *Fiddler on the Roof* is a great work of art. I think the creators of *Fiddler on the Roof* were participants in a Great Conversation about fathers and daughters that stretches all the way back to the Hebrew Bible. I think that *Fiddler on the Roof* is now part of that Great Conversation, and people will still be arguing about *Fiddler on the Roof* in 100 years… and maybe even in 400 years. I think the sources of its power are fairly well known, but most of the synergies which made *Fiddler on the Roof* such a phenomenal—and unexpected—success way back in 1964 have yet to be fully appreciated.

In what follows, I may be 50% correct or 75% correct or 25% correct. My goal is to engage you in a Great Conversation about the sources and synergies of *Fiddler on the Roof*, and if I succeed, then everything I have done since May 20, 2000, will have been worth it.

L'Chaim!

Jan Lisa Huttner
Brooklyn, NY
September 22, 2014

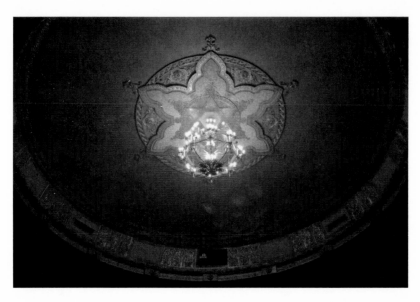

© Jan Lisa Huttner (2013)

© Jan Lisa Huttner (2018)

© Judith Klausner (2010)

Introduction:
From Seven to Five to Three?

Just before season three of the popular British series *Downton Abbey* began airing in the USA, several articles appeared in various publications explicitly comparing *Downton Abbey* to *Fiddler on the Roof*. The mostly widely read was a piece in the January 23, 2012, issue of the *New Yorker*, in which television critic Emily Nussbaum said this:

> I prefer to think of *Downton Abbey* as an experimental take on *Fiddler on the Roof*. Just think of the Earl of Grantham as Tevye, with his three rebel daughters, plus a much better roof. *L'chaim*, m'lord.

Nussbaum was onto something. There is indeed a thread that links *Downton Abbey* to *Fiddler on the Roof*, a connection much deeper than Nussbaum likely knew when she penned her clever bons mots. Yet with so many stories about fathers and daughters to choose from—Shakespeare's *King Lear* being the most obvious one—it is a tribute to the pervasive hold *Fiddler on the Roof* has on the popular imagination that a critic in 2012 would use it as a reference point for a new media darling like *Downton Abbey*.

But everyone who has ever seen *Fiddler on the Roof* knows that Broadway's Tevye had five daughters, not three. And everyone who has ever read *Tevye the Dairyman* knows that Solomon Rabinowitz—the author best known today by his pen name Sholem Aleichem—gave Tevye seven daughters, not five. So how do we go from seven to five to three? That is the subject of this book.

© Manuel Bennett (1992)

SECTION 3

Sholem Aleichem's Daughters: The Family of "Yiddish Tevye"

Fiddler on the Roof is based on a series of stories by the Yiddish author Solomon Rabinowitz (best known by his pen name Sholem Aleichem). Although these eight stories were written between 1895 and 1916, they are typically published today in one book with eight chapters. One hundred years later, *Tevye the Dairyman* occupies a unique place in the history of world literature. Because it was written in real time, this "novel" reflects the actual changes occurring in Eastern Europe from the time that Solomon Rabinowitz was a recently-married young man living in Kiev (Ukraine) until the time he died in the Bronx (New York) in 1916.

Like all of the stories in *Tevye the Dairyman*, chapter one, "The Great Windfall," is a monologue in which a working man named Tevye tells his life story to a writer named Sholem Aleichem. The character "Sholem Aleichem" never speaks, he just listens. It is Tevye who does all the talking.

Tevye's seven daughters are first introduced in an aside. While telling Sholem Aleichem how poor he was before "The Great Windfall" enabled him to become a dairyman, Tevye quotes his wife Golde's lament: "I had to bear him children, and seven at that!" Several pages later, describing his reply to a question from his benefactor, Tevye says:

> Children? I can't complain… Daughters I have.
> And if you have daughters, it's no laughing mat-
> ter. But never mind, God is our father and He
> prevails. (Shevrin, Page 15)

© NCJF (1939)

Why did Rabinowitz choose seven for the number of daughters?

In Jeremy Dauber's 2013 book *The Worlds of Sholem Aleichem: The Remarkable Life and Afterlife of the Man Who Created Tevye*, Dauber suggests an explanation which resonates with the actual way Aliza Shevrin chose to translate the passage above in 2009:

> *Fiddler on the Roof* viewers may be wondering where the extra daughters got to... The reason to start with seven daughters is clearer, though: an old Yiddish saying that "zibn tekhter is keyn gelekhter"—seven daughters is no laughing matter—because, of course, of the seven dowries the father must come up with. Sholem Aleichem seems to have tossed in the detail to simply indicate the kind of financial woes that Tevye has, clothing the proverbial in actual flesh, blending the worlds of imagination and reality. (Dauber, Pages 102-103)

Dauber's concern ends there, but the question remains: Why seven? Wouldn't the "financial woes" be just about the same if the number of daughters were six or eight... ?

Seven is, of course, the number of days in a week; therefore the proverb is a reference to the Jewish Sabbath. God finished His work of creation on the sixth day, and on the seventh day He rested. Then He commanded man to rest on the seventh day as well: "Remember the seventh day and keep it holy." But the father of seven daughters, where is his rest? Even if he does no work on the Sabbath, surely his worries will continue to work on him.

And so, Tevye, a character now beloved by many generations, began his literary life in 1895 with seven daughters. Over time, in subsequent chapters, as Tevye's life unfolded and he told Sholem Aleichem new stories, six of his seven daughters got names (Bielke, Chava, Hodel, Shprintze, Taybele, and Tzeitel), and five of them got stories in which they played lead roles (first Tzeitel, then Hodel, then Chava, then Shprintze, and finally, Bielke). The names of three daughters even became story titles ("Hodel," "Chava," and "Shprintze"). But, alas, poor Taybele never got a story, and the seventh daughter never even got a name.

Later in this book, I will discuss the members of the real Rabinowitz family and ask how life impacted art, but first, let us look at two other fathers, each of whom also had five daughters...

© Greg Kolack (2007)

SECTION 4

Joseph Stein's Daughters:
The Family of "Broadway Tevye"

Prior to the Broadway debut of *Fiddler on the Roof* in 1964, several different adaptations of the Tevye stories appeared on stage and screen in America and beyond. The earliest screen version was an American silent film called *Broken Barriers*. *Broken Barriers*— based on Rabinowitz's own theatrical treatment—was released in 1919 (just a few years after Rabinowitz died). The Internet Movie Database also lists a German film called *Tevya und Seine Tochter* (*Tevye and His Daughters*) from 1962.

After *Fiddler on the Roof* became a Broadway sensation, an Israeli film called *Tuvia Ve Sheva Benotav* (*Tevye and His Seven Daughters*) was released in 1968, as well as two Russian versions *Tevye Molochnik* (*Tevye the Milkman*) in 1985, and *Izydi!* (*Get Thee Out!*) in 1991. I have never seen any of these films myself, and to the best of my knowledge, no one else I know personally has either.

(Update 2018: I saw *Tuvia Ve Sheva Benotav* in 2015. As I say on my blog post: "There is a good reason why *Tuvia Ve Sheva Benotav*, the Israeli version of Sholem Aleichem's Tevye stories, is rarely seen. It doesn't deserve to be. Although of great historical interest to *Fiddler* fanatics like me, it is objectively awful and best kept apocryphal… ")

The pre-*Fiddler on the Roof* adaptation most readily accessible is Maurice Schwartz's film *Tevye*, originally released in 1939, re-released a few years ago by the National Center for Jewish Film, and based on the popular stage version Schwartz created for

31

© Carol Rosegg (2005)

his Yiddish Art Theatre (starring Schwartz himself—of course—as Tevye). The Schwartz version, which is very likely close in content to *Broken Barriers*, focuses primarily on Chava. The only other daughter in the cast is Tzeitel. Perhaps Tevye and Golde are meant to have additional children, but, if so, they are never seen or referred to in Schwartz's version.

Also available in script form from the Dramatists Play Service is Arnold Perl's play, *Tevya and His Daughters*, first produced in New York in 1957. According to page 77 of Alisa Solomon's book, *Wonder of Wonders: A Cultural History of* Fiddler on the Roof, *Tevya and His Daughters* "closed after a six-week run" in New York, nor did it "thrill the provinces as [Perl's earlier play *The World of Sholem Aleichem*] had done."

In all these years since May 2000, I have never heard of anyone reviving *Tevya and His Daughters*, although if the Dramatists Play Service still carries it, then I suppose people somewhere must still consider it as an option. For purposes of this discussion, what is most important is that Perl's script explicitly calls for seven daughters. Tzeitel, Hodel, and Chava all have speaking roles in Perl's script, and then, when Hodel marries Perchik in Act Two:

> ... four small daughters enter, carrying
> a homemade chuppah, or marriage canopy.
> (Perl, Page 41)

Yup. The big ceremony in Perl's version is the wedding of Hodel and Perchik. After their wedding, they tell Tevye that Perchik is leaving. "This is what he has to do," says Hodel on page 42.

Anyway, for legal reasons beyond the scope of this discussion, *Fiddler on the Roof* cast albums continue to carry the words "book by Joseph Stein (based on Sholem Aleichem's stories by special permission of Arnold Perl)," even though Stein—who died in 2010—always denied that he drew from Perl's version.

So why did two of the daughters holding up Perl's chuppah simply vanish between 1957 and 1964? For me, it is not enough to say there were already too many people onstage. If Perl could fit them on a tiny Off-Broadway stage, then why couldn't Stein fit them on a much bigger Broadway stage?

The answer must be that Stein made a deliberate decision to give Tevye five daughters instead of seven, but as far as I know, no one ever asked Stein about this. And even if he had been asked, Stein might have shrugged off a direct question (much as his son Harry Stein did when I asked him this question in September 2013).

In the absence of evidence to the contrary, this mystery becomes an instance of "artistic alchemy"—five just felt right—even if Stein couldn't say why. But we don't have to reach too far to find another famous father who also lacked dowries for his five daughters: meet Mr. Bennet of Longbourn.

© BBC (1995)

Mr. Bennet's Daughters:
The Family in *Pride and Prejudice*

Tevye has five daughters in *Fiddler on the Roof*, and Mr. Bennet—the head of the Longbourn household in Jane Austen's much-loved novel *Pride and Prejudice*—also has five daughters. But why assume Joseph Stein either knew or cared? In fact, there is a missing link.

In 1959, a new musical called *First Impressions* opened on Broadway. Based on *Pride and Prejudice*, *First Impressions* was the creation of Abe Burrows (best known today as the man behind *Guys and Dolls* and *How to Succeed in Business Without Really Trying*). The cover of the French's Musical Library edition published in 1962 calls *First Impressions* "a Musical Comedy adapted by Abe Burrows from Helen Jerome's dramatization of Jane Austen's novel *Pride and Prejudice*, with music and lyrics by Robert Goldman, Glenn Paxton, and George Weiss."

For the record, when Jane Austen wrote her first novel—a novel about the Bennet family of Longbourn—she called it *First Impressions*, but she couldn't find a publisher. However, once *Sense and Sensibility*—Austen's second novel—became a popular success, T. Egerton of Whitehall, the publisher of *Sense and Sensibility*, agreed to release *First Impressions* with a new name: *Pride and Prejudice*. In this early instance of successful branding, a novel called *First Impressions* went nowhere, but given a new title, *Pride and Prejudice* quickly became one of the great classics of Western literature.

Nevertheless, despite Burrows's track record and the participation of well-known stars of the day such as Polly Bergen as "Lizzie," Farley Granger as "Mr. Darcy," and Hermione Gingold in the starring role of "Mrs. Bennet," *First Impressions* was a flop. Passionate Austenites will no doubt cringe at the thought of building an adaptation of *Pride and Prejudice* around the character of Mrs. Bennet (!), but sometimes truth really is stranger than fiction.

Immediately after the overture, Mrs. Bennet sings an opening number called "Five Daughters," and here is how it begins:

> Five daughters
> How did it happen?
> How could I have managed
> To produce five of a kind?

After enumerating all her problems, Mrs. Bennet concludes:

> Five maidens
> Waiting to be mated
> Jane's too shy, too easily hurt
> Lydia's just a frivolous flirt
> Kitty keeps on tagging along
> Mary sings that horrible song
> Lizzie and Lizzie…

> Dear Lord (*Spoken.*)
> We need extra help with Lizzie…
> So much needs to be done
> And if you possibly can
> Please keep her mouth closed. Thank you.

> (*Sung.*)

> Daughters help a home to thrive
> And I've got
> Five! (Burrows, Pages 12-13)

To whom is Mrs. Bennet addressing her spoken recitative? Mrs. Bennet is speaking directly to God ("Dear Lord"); Mrs. Bennet is asking God to personally manage her daughter Lizzie's assertive behavior.

So that's Act One, Scene 1. In Act Two, Scene 2, Mrs. Bennet gets another big solo. It's called "A House in Town," and here is how it begins:

> My poor, poor family… my little dears
> How we've suffered and struggled through these lean lean years
> But I know
> The hand of Providence will one day turn the tide
> And I will be granted
> That wonderful dream
> I've always kept inside
> A house in town
> A house in town
> Just a tiny MMM spectacular
> House in town
> Nothing very much
> Just a smashing house in town

And off Mrs. Bennet goes, fantasizing about life in her new house. And here is how Mrs. Bennet ends her reverie:

> There'll be dancing
> There'll be drinking
> There'll be caviar
> By the ton
> Ach du lieber
> What a triumph
> And the evening's
> Just begun
> Excitement is growing
> The tension is mounting
> The glorious moment is here
>
> (*Spoken.*)
>
> A hush falls over the crowd
> A delicate fanfare, not too long, not too soft
> All eyes will turn to see
> There, poised at the top of the stairs… me
> Gad, she's beautiful! (Burrows, Pages 67-68)

When I first read these words, I was startled. Who could have predicted way back in 1959 that one day Tevyes all around the world would sing about a stairway "leading nowhere just for show"?

Listen to the Original Cast Recording, and there is something even more evocative about the songs Mrs. Bennet sings in *First Impressions* than the words, namely the vocalizations indicated by the "MMM." Five years before Zero Mostel began doing the "deedle-deedle-dums" that punctuate "If I Were a Rich Man," Mrs. Bennet was talking to God and then adding her own "MMM" vocalization while fantasizing about a new house.

To recap: In 1959, Mrs. Bennet, the main character in a Broadway adaptation of Jane Austen's novel *Pride and Prejudice* called *First Impressions*, talked directly to God, vocalized in nonsense syllables, and dreamt about showing herself off at the top of a staircase. All this in a musical about beleaguered parents who have no money for the dowries of their five daughters.

Can I tell you definitively that anyone on the *Fiddler on the Roof* team even knew about *First Impressions*, let alone saw a live performance at some point during the three-month Broadway run? I cannot. But we must remember that all of the members of the *Fiddler on the Roof* team were established Broadway figures by the time they began collaborating on *Fiddler on the Roof*. According to the Internet Broadway Database page for *First Impressions*, Abe Burrows is credited with "Book and Direction," and the musical was produced in association with the Jule Styne Organization. Could consummate professionals like the members of the *Fiddler on the Roof* team have been totally oblivious to a new work by such major competitors? Not likely.

Now, you may ask: Given the legions of passionate Jane Austen fans, why has *First Impressions* vanished from popular consciousness? I'll tell you: I don't know. But here are a couple of speculations.

© Sony (1959)

First of all, even though Hermione Gingold had just won the Golden Globe in the Best Supporting Actress category in 1958 for her role in the film version of *Gigi*, building an adaptation of *Pride and Prejudice* around the character of Mrs. Bennet was probably ill-advised from the start. And Polly Bergen—who played Lizzie, was a very beautiful woman—but she really wasn't much of a singer. That said, I think the real reason it disappeared so fast is because *Gypsy* opened right behind it.

First Impressions opened while *My Fair Lady* was in the middle of a very lengthy run. (*My Fair Lady* opened in March 1956 and it closed in September 1962.) Clearly both of these shows were high-pedigree adaptations of British classics. My guess is that the success of *My Fair Lady* helped investors warm to the idea of doing another show somewhat like it, and that gave the *First Impressions* team a leg up.

But then *Gypsy* opened on May 21, 1959… and *First Impressions* closed soon after (on May 30). Coincidence? I do not think so. However good Hermione Gingold might have been in *First Impressions*, the reviews for *Gypsy* were extraordinary, and *Gypsy* is now considered one of the greatest musicals in Broadway history. So if you wanted to go British, you likely chose Julie Andrews in *My Fair Lady*, and if you wanted to see a mother singing about her daughters, you likely picked Ethel Merman in *Gypsy*. When *Gypsy* opened on May 21, *First Impressions* was done.

Now accept for a moment that the number five "felt right" to Joseph Stein if only because he knew that *Pride and Prejudice* was a popular novel that had already been adapted for both stage and screen. So he sensed—consciously or not—that a story about five daughters in a new musical might resonate with his own potential audience members.

Why did Jane Austen choose the number five? The answer is in the Bible.

The Book of Numbers is the fourth of the five Books of Moses which comprise the Hebrew "Old Testament." By the end of the Book of Numbers, right before the start of the Book of Deuteronomy, Jacob's descendants have wandered in the desert for forty years. But before they can take possession of the Promised Land, they must first deal with the issue of allocation: who will settle where?

© Friedman-Abeles (1959)

© Iris Wexler (1985)

SECTION 6

Zelophehad's Daughters: The Family in the Book of Numbers

The Israelites have been divided into Twelve Tribes of Israel for each of the sons of Jacob, and the clans of each tribe are to receive one share. Descended from Jacob's son Joseph (through the line of Joseph's son Manasseh) is Zelophehad, but in Numbers 26:33, "Zelophehad, son of Hepher, had no sons, only daughters."

(Update 2018: If Jacob has twelve sons who all become heads of tribes, but then Joseph's two sons become heads of tribes, then technically there are 13 tribes. But land is only allocated to 12 of the tribes because the Tribe of Levi has a special function. As priests they get no land; rather they get sprinkled around the lands of their brethren. It was only late in the proofreading phase that I even thought to ask myself about this obvious discrepancy in the definition of the "Twelve Tribes.")

> The daughters of Zelophehad, of Manassite family—son of Hepher, son of Gilead, son of Machir, son of Manasseh, son of Joseph—came forward. The names of the daughters were **Mahlah, No'ah, Hoglah, Milcah, and Tirzah.** They stood before Moses, Eleazar the priest, the chieftains, and the whole assembly, at the entrance of the Tent of Meeting, and they said, "Our father died in the wilderness… Let not our father's name be lost to his clan just because he had no son! Give us a holding among our father's kinsmen!" (Numbers 27:1-4)
>
> And Moses brought their case before the Lord; and the Lord said to Moses, "The plea of Zelophehad's daughters is just. You should give

them a hereditary holding among their father's kinsmen; transfer their father's share to them." (Numbers 27:5–7)

Further speak to the Israelite people as follows: "If a man dies without leaving a son, you shall transfer his property to his daughter. This shall be the law of procedure for the Israelites in accordance with the Lord's command to Moses." (Numbers 27:8–11)

Of course there is some subsequent pushback from Zelophehad's kinsmen and a few new restrictions are placed on his daughters.

So Moses, at the Lord's bidding, instructed the Israelites, saying: "The plea of the Josephite tribe is just. This is what the Lord has commanded concerning the daughters of Zelophehad: 'They may marry anyone they wish, provided they marry into a clan of their father's tribe. No inheritance of the Israelites may pass over from one tribe to another, but the Israelites must remain bound each to the ancestral portion of his tribe. Every daughter among the Israelite tribes who inherits a share must marry someone from a clan of her father's tribe, in order that every Israelite may keep his ancestral share. Thus no inheritance shall pass over from one tribe to another, but the Israelite tribes shall remain bound each to its portion.'"(Numbers 33:1–36:13)

What is most significant to me in this story is that the five daughters of Zelophehad—Mahlah, No'ah, Hoglah, Milcah, and Tirzah—are all listed by name—as individuals—first in chapter 26, and then again in chapter 27. And they are all mentioned by name just before the Book of Numbers ends with one final line: "These are the commandments and regulations that the Lord enjoined upon the Israelites, through Moses, on the steppes of Moab, at the Jordan near Jericho." (Numbers 36:13)

Did Jane Austen know the story of the daughters of Zelophehad? Did she know about these five bold women who "stood before Moses, Eleazar the priest, the chieftains, and the whole assembly, at the entrance of the Tent of Meeting" ? Five women who are known to us by their own names—as individuals—and therefore not just as a group known collectively as the daughters of their father Zelophehad?

How could she not? This is not some obscure prophet speaking. This is in the climax to the Book of Numbers (when Moses is allocating the land God had promised to Abraham), in a part of the Bible that every well-educated person in Austen's time would have been expected to know.

Jane Austen was the bookish daughter of an Anglican rector, and references to the Bible appear in all recent books about her. Even the readers of the book *Jane Austen for Dummies* know this from page 76:

> As the daughter of an Anglican clergyman, Austen read the Bible in the King James Version and the Book of Common Prayer… practically required reading for all young people of the gentry class (particularly if your father was a clergyman).

So why are there almost no references to Zelophehad's daughters in publications about Jane Austen? I attribute this to the very same patriarchal pushback Moses encountered from Zelophehad's kinsmen, augmented by a lack of familiarity in our current time with the biblical text.

Why did Zelophehad have five daughters? Only God knows the answer to this question. But we can be sure that both Jane Austen and Solomon Rabinowitz had read the story of Zelophehad's five daughters, and it is highly likely that Joseph Stein had read it at one time too. The number five is the right number; it gets its resonance from the very top. And as we will shall see below, five daughters—or to be exact, five dowries—is the same number God also bestowed upon Solomon Rabinowitz.

© YIVO Archives (circa 1890)

Solomon Rabinowitz's Daughters: The Family that Once Lived in Kiev

As I explained earlier, the eight Tevye stories, when collected and published together, become a "novel" written in real time. The author who wrote "The Great Windfall" in 1895 witnessed many momentous world events in the course of his life, but amidst the wars, pogroms, and Zionist Congresses, he also lived a "real" life. Sholem Aleichem was an author, but Solomon Rabinowitz was also a son, a husband, and a father. However, even with all the interest in this man since his death in 1916—a death that occasioned an outpouring of grief all across the Yiddish-speaking world and led to one of the largest funeral parades ever seen in the city of New York—there has been amazingly little examination of his family life.

"I have five daughters," brays Tevye in the opening moments of *Fiddler on the Roof.* "I have five daughters!" And yet, even having heard these four words ("I have five daughters!") dozens of times, it wasn't until August 2011 (just before my third annual lecture on *Fiddler on the Roof* for the Chicago YIVO Society), that I suddenly thought to ask myself a very simple question: "Mmmm, I wonder if Solomon Rabinowitz had any daughters?"

Perhaps people assume that with such a flood of literary treasures, Rabinowitz didn't have time for much else, but the reality is quite different. Marie Waife-Goldberg laid out all the details in her book *My Father, Sholom Aleichem* (published in 1968). Nevertheless, even recent books like Jeremy Dauber's *The Worlds of Sholem Aleichem*—which is 448 pages long—continue to minimize the importance of Rabinowitz's family life.

However, with Marie Waife-Goldberg as our guide, a fairly coherent story is readily available about the Rabinowitz family… and the historical record clearly shows that for the purposes of a *Fiddler on the Roof* aficionado like me, Solomon Rabinowitz… had… five… daughters! And here is how it all came to be.

Solomon Rabinowitz was born into a relatively prosperous family. His father was a scholar and his mother ran the business, which was typical for a Jewish family in that place at that time. They had many children (some have said as many as 11 or 12), and Mama Rabinowitz—Chaya Esther—raised them all, while Papa Rabinowitz—Reb Nochem Vevik—did his thing.

Then Papa Rabinowitz made some bad business decisions and basically bankrupted the family. They were forced to leave their home and soon after that, just after Solomon's Bar Mitzvah, Mama Rabinowitz—Chaya Esther—died. Papa Rabinowitz—Reb Nochem Vevik—was not able to care for his many children, so he dispersed them, calling the children back home one by one, after he remarried. But his second wife was none too pleased about this, and she basically forced them out of the house again.

And so at the very young age of 14 or 15, Solomon Rabinowitz was making a living as an itinerant teacher—and it was a very marginal living indeed. In his autobiography *From the Fair*, Rabinowitz tells stories about his various adventures, most of which are heartbreaking, as he wandered alone in the world.

Then one day Rabinowitz met a young man named Joshua Loyeff. Joshua was the son of a very wealthy man named Elimelech Loyeff, and after talking with Rabinowitz for a while, Joshua arranged a meeting. Once Elimelech Loyeff met Rabinowitz, he decided to bring him back to his estate in Sofievka (now Ukraine). In the daytime, Rabinowitz was to work as a children's tutor, and in the evening, Rabinowitz was to help with correspondence and other things that might need doing to manage the large Loyeff estate.

LOYEFF FAMILY TREE

© Jan Lisa Huttner (2018)

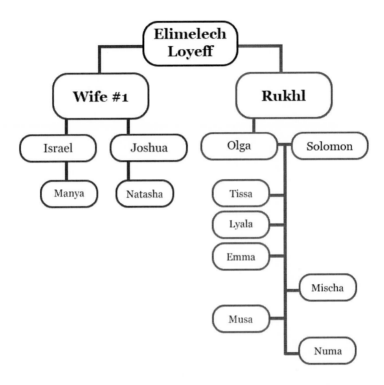

Who did Rabinowitz find on the Loyeff estate in Sofievka when he arrived there in 1877 at the age of 18?

Well, Elimelech Loyeff had two wives. We don't know the name of his first wife. All we know is that she gave birth to two sons—Israel and Joshua—and then she died. Sometime after his first wife died, Elimelech Loyeff married a woman named Rachel (Rukhl) Yampolsky. In the fullness of time, Rachel gave birth to a daughter named Olga.

Israel and Joshua eventually married too; they each had one daughter and then they both divorced. The mothers of these two little girls—also nameless—disappeared, so alongside her own

49

daughter Olga, Rachel also cared for Manya and Natasha (who were technically her step-granddaughters).

So when Solomon Rabinowitz arrived in Sofievka, the children in the household were, in fact, three girls:

- Olga (age 15)
- Manya (age 9)
- Natasha (age 5)

Eventually Olga's parents realized that their daughter had fallen in love with her tutor, so Rabinowitz was turned out. Elimelech Loyeff made sure that Rabinowitz was denied access to Olga, confiscating all the letters Rabinowitz tried to send to her. But Olga refused to marry anyone else, and eventually she found him again. Solomon and Olga married in 1883.

Sadly, both of Olga's step brothers were dead by this point, so Elimelech Loyeff accepted Solomon Rabinowitz into his home as a son. Then, in 1885, two years after the marriage, Elimelech Loyeff died. According to Russian property laws, women could not inherit, and so his vast fortune went to Solomon Rabinowitz, and the two teenage girls—Manya and Natasha—who were probably once his students became his legal wards.

Solomon and Olga had their first child—a daughter named Ernestina—in 1884. (They called her Tissa at home.) Daughter Lyala was born in 1887, the same year that Manya died of tuberculosis at age 19. A third daughter—Emma—was born in 1888. In 1889, Olga finally gave birth to a son. They named him Elimelech, after Olga's father, but at home they called him Misha. Maroussia (called Musa at home)—who would one day publish *My Father, Sholom Aleichem* under her married name Marie Waife-Goldberg—was born in 1892. A final child, a son named Nochum after Solomon's father, but called Numa at home, was born in 1901. (Numa became a well-known painter in America under the name Norman Raeben.)

RABINOWITZ FAMILY TREE

© Jan Lisa Huttner (2018)

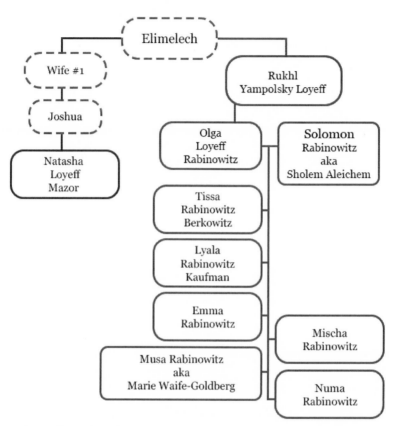

Technically Solomon and Olga Rabinowitz had six children—four daughters and two sons—but the full reality is that Rabinowitz was responsible for the dowries of five girls: Natasha, Tissa, Lyala, Emma, and Musa. Calling himself "Your Loving Uncle" in subsequent letters to Natasha (after her marriage to a much older man) likely did little to lessen the emotional burden he carried. This was definitely "no laughing matter," because in 1890, Rabinowitz lost all of Elimelech Loyeff's money in a stock market crash. He was rescued by his mother-in-law Rachel Yampolsky, who pawned her jewelry and other household possessions to pay off his creditors.

He worried about the fate of "his children"—including Natasha—for the rest of his life.

Putting all of this together, I kept asking myself: "Can this really be right?" If yes, then why hadn't anyone connected these dots before? After all, all of this information is in *My Father, Sholom Aleichem* (which Musa had published under the name Marie Waife-Goldberg way back in 1968). This family history is also encapsulated in *Our Sholem Aleichem*, a biography published in 1946 "on the occasion of the centenary of the birth of Sholem Aleichem" by Kinderbook Publications in New York.

Most of it is also contained in *Sholem Aleichem Panorama*, published by the Jewish Observer Media in Canada in 1948. This gorgeous tribute—which is over 400 pages long—is filled with photographs and sketches, and also includes first-person reports by Lyala (writing under the name Lala Kaufman), Musa (writing under the name Marie W. Goldberg), and Tissa's husband Isaac (writing under the name I.D. Berkowitz). *Sholem Aleichem Panorama* even includes a piece called "Madame Sholom Aleichem" by Regina Mantell. (Olga Loyeff Rabinowitz had passed away in 1942.) Regina Mantell also mentions Olga's Yiddish name in her piece, repeatedly referring to her as "young Hodl."

The lines are as follows:

> In the history of literature there are instances
> of the wife who serves as a continual source of
> stimulation and inspiration to the genius of her
> writer husband. Such a wife was Olga-Hodl.
> Not only did she inspire and stimulate the
> youthful Sholom Rabinowitz, but in later years
> as Madame Sholom Aleichem she created the
> proper atmosphere around the great Sholom
> Aleichem. (Grafstein, Page 219)

Nevertheless, these family details fly right by Jeremy Dauber, whose book *The Worlds of Sholem Aleichem*, which includes extensive quotes from *My Father, Sholom Aleichem*, was published in October 2013. Looking in Wikipedia today, yet again I see that none of the daughters are named except Lyala (and only because she is the mother of the recently-deceased writer Bel Kaufman). And the Yiddish name given for Madame Sholem Aleichem today —in Wikipedia—is… Golde! No one but me, it seems, has any interest in the role women played in the real Rabinowitz family.

But suddenly, knowing what I know now, I re-read *Tevye the Dairyman* with new eyes, and I find that a master storyteller has embedded pieces of his own life into the plot points of his most famous stories.

Am I implying that what we know about Solomon Rabinowitz's family life can be mapped onto the plot of *Fiddler on the Roof* ? Yes. Conventional Wisdom is that the *Fiddler on the Roof* team got it all wrong. But when Joseph Stein decided that the number of daughters had to be five, I think he got closer to the core of Sholem Aleichem's art than anyone has ever realized.

© Carnival (2010)

SECTION 8

Earl of Grantham's Daughters: The Family in *Downton Abbey*

We have now made our way from the seven unnamed daughters alluded to in the first Tevye story ("The Great Windfall") down to the five named daughters seen on stage in *Fiddler on the Roof*. We have also met the five daughters of Zelophehad (from the Book of Numbers) and the five Bennet daughters in *Pride and Prejudice* (as well as the five daughters in the Broadway adaptation of *Pride and Prejudice* called *First Impressions*), all of whom also have names. So why are there only three daughters in *Downton Abbey*?

When I ask people why Tevye only has five daughters in *Fiddler on the Roof* even though he says he has seven daughters in "The Great Windfall," they usually tell me the change must have been driven by dollars: it was easier and cheaper to have five girls on stage rather than seven.

But that answer has never satisfied me. As I have already said, Arnold Perl managed to fit all seven girls on a tiny Off-Broadway stage, so Joseph Stein could surely have fit them somewhere on a Broadway stage too if he felt his libretto required them. (In Act One of *The King and I*, which opened on Broadway in 1951, Rodgers and Hammerstein brought a whole gaggle of kids onto the stage for "The March of the Siamese Children," and they've been part of every production ever since.)

But the truth is that only three of the daughters in *Fiddler on the Roof* actually take on active roles that drive the plot forward. Shprintze and Bielke are presented as children, too young to be fully individuated. Is it a coincidence that in film versions of *Pride and Prejudice* (as well as in *First Impressions*), Mary and Kitty—the middle Bennet daughters—also live on the sidelines?

Therefore to tighten the plot, and make room for all of the action they wanted to add down in the servant's quarters, the creators of *Downton Abbey* decided to give the Earl of Grantham three daughters—Lady Mary Crawley, Lady Edith Crawley and Lady Sybil Crawley—instead of five. No one writing about the parallels between *Fiddler on the Roof* and *Downton Abbey* seems to have noticed anyone missing.

But the widely-televised depiction of Lady Mary's fate as the eldest daughter of a titled father who has no sons has hit England hard. Go online and you will find a group called "The Hares" campaigning for the Equality (Titles) Bill, "a change in the law to end male primogeniture and bring equality to women in the peerage."

The Hares sprang into action as soon as Parliament passed the Succession to the Crown Act of 2013 "a landmark bill to end the centuries-old discrimination against women in line to the British throne." (This happened right after Prince William's wife—Kate Middleton, the Duchess of Cambridge—announced her pregnancy, and before she gave birth to the newest Prince George.) The December 9, 2013, issue of the *New Yorker* referred to "The Equality (Titles) Bill now being debated in the House of Lords" as "the so-called *Downton Abbey* law."

Thus we have come full circle, from *Downton Abbey* to *Fiddler on the Roof* to *Pride and Prejudice* through *First Impressions* to the Book of Numbers, and from the complicated personal life of the real Solomon Rabinowitz back to the lords of the manor who live in today's England.

And if we were to remind members of the House of Lords that in chapter 27 of the Book of Numbers "the Lord said to Moses, 'The plea of Zelophehad's daughters is just,'" what would they say? That I can answer in one word: Tradition! Lady Mary Crawley be damned. Jane Austen be damned. Moses be damned. Primogeniture is our English tradition.

© Rob Copeland (2018)

© Eileen Darby Images, Inc. (1964)

Concluding Thoughts: Tradition? Traditions?

"Tradition." Tradition! Tradition? At the beginning of *Fiddler on the Roof*, during what is called the Musical-Prologue, everyone sings about "Tradition." But that is where *Fiddler on the Roof* begins, not where it ends.

Here is one example of the complexity inherent in the word tradition: How should Jews celebrate Hanukkah?

What are the "traditional" foods of Hanukkah? For most Jewish Americans (most of whom come from Ashkenazi families), the answer is latkes. For most Jewish Israelis (most of whom come from Mizrahi families), the answer is donuts. But the people eating donuts and the people eating latkes, they are all still Jews. So what are the "traditional" foods of Hanukkah? If you are Jewish, then the "traditional" foods of Hanukkah are probably the ones your grandmother made.

And what are the "traditional" songs of Hanukkah? For Jews living in the USA (which is an Anglophone country), the favorite song is probably "Oh Hanukkah, Oh Hanukkah, Come Light the Menorah" (which is based on a Yiddish song). But for Jews living in Argentina (which is a Hispanophone country), the favorite song is probably "Ocho Kandelikas" (which is in Ladino). But the people singing "Oh Hanukkah, Oh Hanukkah" and the people singing "Ocho Kandelikas," they are all still Jews. So what are the "traditional" songs of Hanukkah? If you are Jewish, then the "traditional" songs of Hanukkah are probably the ones your grandmother sang.

When it comes right down to it, Jewish Americans don't even agree on how to spell this Hebrew word in English. But if I spell it H-A-N-U-K-K-A-H and you spell it C-H-A-N-U-K-A-H, we can still eat fried foods and sing holiday songs together.

"Tradition" is not an answer with a capital "T" at the beginning; "tradition" is a question with a small "s" at the end. There are many Jewish traditions, and they are all valid Jewish traditions. So that means individual Jews have choices to make. If you choose cards that spell the holiday H-A-N-U-K-K-A-H in English, that doesn't make you any more Jewish or any less Jewish than choosing cards that spell the holiday C-H-A-N-U-K-A-H.

The creators of *Fiddler on the Roof*, all of whom were Jewish, grew up in a syncretic American world, so they picked out various Jewish traditions and then they dramatized them. But that does not mean they picked out the "best" Jewish traditions, and when it suited their dramatic purposes, they even made up "traditions."

For example, when I told you about Solomon Rabinowitz's daughters in "The Family that Once Lived in Kiev," you never heard me mention the word "matchmaker," did you? That's because matchmakers were not as ubiquitous as the creators of *Fiddler on the Roof* would have you believe.

Here are the daughters' lyrics from the Musical-Prologue:

> And who does Mama teach
> To mend and tend and fix,
> Preparing me to marry
> Whoever Papa picks? (Stein, Page 4)

For 50 years now, we have been led to believe that these lyrics are an accurate representation of "Tradition!"—with a capital "T" and an exclamation point—as lived in the Russian Jewish world at the turn of the 20th century. But when we look at the actual lives of the two men who created the source material for *Fiddler on the Roof*, we find that it just isn't so.

The man known as "Sholem Aleichem"—the man whose real name was Solomon Rabinowitz—was married to a woman named

Olga Loyeff. Olga Loyeff's father—Elimelech Loyeff—was very wealthy; Solomon Rabinowitz was penniless. Elimelech Loyeff hired Solomon Rabinowitz as a tutor, and he also expected him to assist with various secretarial tasks. So Solomon Rabinowitz lived on the Loyeff estate in a service role. He wasn't washing dishes, but he was still an employee.

Elimelech Loyeff undoubtedly had grand designs for his daughter Olga. Elimelech Loyeff emphatically did not want Solomon Rabinowitz as his son-in-law. But Olga Loyeff fell in love with Solomon Rabinowitz, and even though her father separated them, she found him. Olga Loyeff and Solomon Rabinowitz got married on May 20, 1883, and they remained together until the day he died on May 13, 1916.

Furthermore, there is no Yente-the-Matchmaker in any of the eight Tevye stories. There is a matchmaker named Ephraim, but he plays a very limited role in the Tevye stories, and he has no power or influence whatsoever. So there is no pivotal matchmaker either in the life of Solomon Rabinowitz or in the stories of Sholem Aleichem. (Note that my thoughts on the character Yente-the-Matchmaker—which are voluminous—must wait for another day.)

And what about Marc and Bella Chagall? Like Olga Loyeff, Bella Rosenberg came from a prosperous family, whereas Marc Chagall, like Solomon Rabinowitz, was penniless. In his autobiography *My Life*, Marc Chagall tells stories of his father carrying barrels of herring. His family had nothing, but Marc Chagall won a scholarship to go to art school. Then he met Bella Rosenberg, a well-educated young woman who wanted to be an actress.

Once again, this was not the match that Bella Rosenberg's father imagined for his daughter. But Bella Rosenberg fell in love with Marc Chagall, and in addition to becoming his wife and the mother of their daughter Ida, she was also his muse. There are many iconic paintings of her, often in a striking black dress with a bright white collar, and famous ones of them together—head-over-heels in love with one another—flying high above their hometown of Vitebsk (now in Belarus). Bella Rosenberg was Marc Chagall's wife. She was his muse. She was the mother of his child. She traveled with him everywhere. She kept him going even in the darkest days of the Holocaust.

Did either of these two couples—the Chagalls or the Rabinowitzes—have a matchmaker? In one of the monologues Joseph Stein wrote for Act Two of *Fiddler on the Roof*, Tevye says:

> Did Adam and Eve have a matchmaker?
> Yes, they did. Then it seems these two
> have the same matchmaker. (Stein, Page 113)

This reference to Hodel and Perchik will not be found in any of the Tevye stories, but they are true to the married life of Olga Loyeff and Solomon Rabinowitz, and also true to the married life of Bella Rosenberg and Marc Chagall. Coincidence?

So what is tradition? Who makes the matches? Should people who want to marry each other be allowed to make this choice? Of all the principal members of *Fiddler on the Roof*'s original creative team—including Boris Aronson, Jerry Bock, Sheldon Harnick, Joseph Stein—only one person was unable to marry for love.

So where would Jerome Robbins stand on the issue of "traditional marriage" if he were alive today? I doubt he would be waving any banners for "tradition." In fact, every time I hear someone talking about "traditional marriage," I can see Jerome Robbins do another flip in his grave.

The literal words of the Hebrew Bible favor the marriage of choice. "Moses, at the Lord's bidding, instructed the Israelites, saying: 'This is what the Lord has commanded concerning the daughters of Zelophehad: They may marry anyone they wish…'"

Of course some restrictions follow, but even so, these radical words—"they may marry anyone they wish"—were first written down over 2,000 years ago. And they continue to be read every year whenever a Jewish congregation anywhere in the world observes Shabbat Mattot/Mas'ei (Numbers 33:1–36:13).

I believe that Jane Austen and Solomon Rabinowitz both knew what the Lord had commanded concerning Mahlah, No'ah, Hoglah, Milcah, and Tirzah—the five named daughters of Zelophehad—and I think Joseph Stein did too (even if he had no conscious memory of the daughters themselves). I feel certain that they all rejected backward—and in this context non-biblical—traditions. In each case, they took their own characters forward into a world of ever more expansive personal choice.

Tradition! Tradition? "Tradition" does not end the story of Tevye and his daughters; traditions were just the beginning.

© Huttner & Rosenzweig (2018)

SECTION 10 - APPENDIX ONE

D'VAR TORAH

Shabbat Pinchas

Numbers 25:10–30:1

Date: July 11, 2014
Place: Temple Beth Emeth (Brooklyn, NY)
Time: 8:30 PM

Tonight we read from Parsha Pinchas which is in the Book of Numbers.

We are in that part of the Torah, on the steppes of Moab, at the Jordan near Jericho, where "the Lord said to Moses and to Eleazar son of Aaron the priest, 'Take a census of the whole Israelite community from the age of twenty years up, by their ancestral houses, all Israelites able to bear arms.'"

When we reach the Descendants of Manasseh (the son of Joseph), the text says:

> Now Zelophehad son of Hepher had no sons, only daughters. The names of Zelophehad's daughters were Mahlah, No'ah, Hoglah, Milcah, and Tirzah.

A few paragraphs later, we read these names again:

> The daughters of Zelophehad, of Manassite family—son of Hepher, son of Gilead, son of Machir, son of Manasseh, son of Joseph—came forward. The names of the daughters were Mahlah, No'ah, Hoglah, Milcah, and Tirzah.

They stood before Moses, Eleazar the priest,
the chieftains, and the whole assembly, at the
entrance of the Tent of Meeting, and they said,
"Our father died in the wilderness. He was
not one of the faction, Korah's faction, which
banded together against the Lord, but died for
his own sin; and he has left no sons. Let not
our father's name be lost to his clan just because
he had no son! Give us a holding among our
father's kinsmen!"

Moses brought their case before the Lord. And
the Lord said to Moses, "The plea of Zelophehad's daughters is just: you should give them a
hereditary holding among their father's kinsmen;
transfer their father's share to them."

Further, speak to the Israelite people as follows:
"If a man dies without leaving a son, you shall
transfer his property to his daughter."

The first thing I want to say about this is that I only found
out about the Daughters of Zelophehad a couple of years ago. As
a lifelong Jewish Feminist, I thought I knew the women of the
Torah pretty well. But somehow I don't remember hearing anyone talk about the Daughters of Zelophehad before overhearing a
snippet of conversation about them one day when I was waiting
for my husband Richard while he was in Torah Study.

And for all my research on *Fiddler on the Roof*, which by that
time had been going on for almost a decade, no one ever thought
to tell me there were five daughters mentioned multiple times by
name in the Book of Numbers!!!

Now I realize that the discussion in this parsha is focused on
male genealogy. In fact, the whole paragraph I read from above is
as follows:

Further, speak to the Israelite people as follows:
"If a man dies without leaving a son, you shall
transfer his property to his daughter. If he has
no daughter, you shall assign his property to his

brothers. If he has no brothers, you shall assign his property to his father's brothers. If his father had no brothers, you shall assign his property to his nearest relative in his own clan, and he shall inherit it." This shall be the law of procedure for the Israelites, in accordance with the Lord's command to Moses.

But still, any woman who has read her Jane Austen must surely be startled:

> And the Lord said to Moses, "The plea of Zelophehad's daughters is just: you should give them a hereditary holding among their father's kinsmen; transfer their father's share to them.
>
> Further, speak to the Israelite people as follows: If a man dies without leaving a son, you shall transfer his property to his daughter."

Wow! And just think of the sheer chutzpah of these daughters: "They stood before Moses, Eleazar the priest, the chieftains, and the whole assembly, at the entrance of the Tent of Meeting, and they said 'Give us a holding among our father's kinsmen!'"

Wow again!

Of course there is some subsequent pushback. A few chapters later, in Parsha Mas'ei, the story of the Daughters of Zelophehad ends as follows:

> The family heads in the clan of the descendants of Gilead, son of Machir, son of Manasseh, one of the Josephite clans, came forward and appealed to Moses and the chieftains, family heads of the Israelites. They said, "The Lord commanded my lord to assign the land to the Israelites as shares by lot, and my lord was further commanded by the Lord to assign the share of our kinsman Zelophehad to his daughters.
>
> Now, if they marry persons from another Israelite tribe, their share will be cut off from our

ancestral portion and be added to the portion of the tribe into which they marry; thus our allotted portion will be diminished. And even when the Israelites observe the jubilee, their share will be added to that of the tribe into which they marry, and their share will be cut off from the ancestral portion of our tribe."

So Moses, at the Lord's bidding, instructed the Israelites, saying: "The plea of the Josephite tribe is just. This is what the Lord has commanded concerning the daughters of Zelophehad: They may marry anyone they wish, provided they marry into a clan of their father's tribe. No inheritance of the Israelites may pass over from one tribe to another, but the Israelites must remain bound each to the ancestral portion of his tribe. Every daughter among the Israelite tribes who inherits a share must marry someone from a clan of her father's tribe, in order that every Israelite may keep his ancestral share. Thus no inheritance shall pass over from one tribe to another, but the Israelite tribes shall remain bound each to its portion."

The daughters of Zelophehad did as the Lord had commanded Moses: Mahlah, Tirzah, Hoglah, Milcah, and No'ah, Zelophehad's daughters, were married to sons of their uncles, marrying into clans of descendants of Manasseh son of Joseph; and so their share remained in the tribe of their father's clan.

These are the commandments and regulations that the Lord enjoined upon the Israelites, through Moses, on the steppes of Moab, at the Jordan near Jericho.

But here are two things I want you to notice. First, all five names are to be read three times—Mahlah, Tirzah, Hoglah, Milcah, and No'ah—so they are known to us as individuals and not just as the daughters of a father whose name was Zelophehad.

And second, Moses specifically says: "They may marry anyone they wish, provided they marry into a clan of their father's tribe."

These women, and the women after them, have the property, so the power to choose remains in their hands… at least until they make a choice of husband.

This is not what we were told was our "Tradition" in *Fiddler on the Roof*, where the daughters explicitly say: "And who does Mama teach, to mend and tend and fix, preparing me to marry whoever Papa picks?"

So my reading of the story of the Daughters of Zelophehad has lead me to ask, once again: Who decides? We can find so many things written in the Torah, and yet even while claiming to be guided only by Scripture, some people take it on themselves to decide that some teachings are more important than others.

Take Gay Marriage, for example. To many it is an anathema. Why? Because homosexual relations are prohibited in the Bible. Some people would have other people killed, or at least imprisoned, because they are homosexuals. Why? Because it's in the Bible.

Horne and Brewer (1908)

But it's perfectly fine to disempower women and rob them of their patrimony, even though that's not only "in the Bible," it is said to be HaShem talking directly to Moses: "And the Lord said to Moses, 'The plea of Zelophehad's daughters is just!'"

Yet even now, a group in England called the Hares is trying to overturn the rules by which property is passed down in moneyed British families. They have brought what they call "Lady Mary's Case" (in honor of Lady Mary Crawley of *Downton Abbey*) to the House of Lords... but so far, no one seems to care...

Last week, we learned about Balaam's donkey. Harmenszoon van Rijn Rembrandt did a famous painting about this creature and rightly so. But why didn't he (or any other famous male painter for that matter) choose the Daughters of Zelophehad— who are mentioned three times by name—as a fit subject?

I leave that to you as an Open Question for discussion at tonight's Oneg Shabbat.

Shabbat Shalom.

D'var Torah

Shabbat Mattot/Mas'ei

Numbers 33:1–36:13

Date: July 15, 2017
Place: Park Slope Jewish Center (Brooklyn, NY)
Time: 12:30 PM

My D'var Torah today on Parsha Pinchas is about "cherry picking," a subject which immediately leads us into the conceptual thicket of memory and the construction of memory—not just how we as individuals construct memories, but how we as a culture construct memories. How do some ideas rather than other ideas become part of what is considered Conventional Wisdom?

Of course, there are a lot of current events we could talk about in this context: faux news, fake news, et cetera, but I don't want to address any of that today. For me to do so in the context of a D'var Torah would be "above my pay grade."

But as many of you already know, I am a professional film critic, so whatever the subject, I always have a movie reference ready to hand…

Who here has seen John Ford's film *The Man Who Shot Liberty Valance* from 1962?

The Man Who Shot Liberty Valance is the story of a very prominent man named "Ransom Stoddard" (played by Jimmy Stewart) who returns home after many years as a man of the world. He's been a congressman. He's been a senator. He's even been the ambassador to Britain's Court of St. James. So, of course, the local press wants an interview with him, and they are especially eager to know all the details about the event that made him famous—the day he shot a really bad dude named Liberty Valance.

SPOILER ALERT: At the end of the interview, Ransom Stoddard reveals—after all these years—that he is not, in fact, the man who shot Liberty Valance. Liberty Valance was killed by "Tom Doniphon" (played by John Wayne). Ransom Stoddard, now at the end of his life, wants to set the record straight… but the publisher does not want to hear it. Then the publisher grabs the pad of paper on which his reporter has been taking notes, and he tears the pages off the pad, and he rips them up!

Ransom Stoddard says: "You're not going to use the story, Mr. Scott?"

And the publisher says: "No, sir. This is the West, sir. When the legend becomes fact, print the legend."

These words are now part of Conventional Wisdom (at least in America):

"When the legend becomes fact, print the legend."

✡ ✡ ✡ ✡ ✡

I really don't know when I first read the story of the five Daughters of Zelophehad—Mahlah, No'ah, Hoglah, Milcah, and Tirzah—probably my sophomore year of college, but who knows? However, I can tell you the exact moment when the story of these five women became personally important to me.

Thinking about this moment now, at the age of 65, I marvel at the fact that I was over 60 before I embraced them. After all, I had been a "feminist" since before Feminism had a name… and a full-fledged Second Wave Warrior. So why did it take me so long to understand how important Mahlah, No'ah, Hoglah, Milcah, and Tirzah should be to me as a Jewish Feminist?

The answer is actually quite simple. The Daughters of Zelophehad had never been cherry-picked. In fact, for most of my adult life, Mahlah, No'ah, Hoglah, Milcah, and Tirzah had been disappeared. They had been disappeared, even though their story is told over two parshot (Pinchas and Mattot/Mas'ei). They had been disappeared, even though they are mentioned multiple times in the Torah by name, meaning not just as the collective "Daughters of Zelophehad." They were simply not part of Conventional Wisdom, neither in my Jewish world nor in my secular world.

Skip to 2011, when my husband Richard began attending Torah Study every month at Congregation KAM Isaiah Israel in Chicago. I went to Services with him, of course, but I did not attend Torah Study because we don't think that as a couple we need to do everything together lockstep. Me? I preferred to spend that time reading quietly by myself, as I do now on the days that Richard attends Talmud Class here at PSJC.

So on that day in July 2012 when members of KAM were studying Parsha Pinchas, I was sitting in a little lounge near the room where the Torah Study class was meeting. I was reading whatever I was reading… when I suddenly became aware of the fact that people in Torah Study were talking about a man with five daughters.

By that point, I had been doing research on *Fiddler on the Roof* for over a decade and I was stunned. When Richard came out of Torah Study, I confronted him: "You were just discussing a Biblical story about a man with five daughters and you didn't think to tell me that was your assignment for this week?" (You can just imagine!)

Richard shrugged: "Nope. Never occurred to me." So, of course, I went back and read the whole parsha, plus the next one, and the following week I was ready to talk to our Rabbi—Rabbi Appel—at Kiddush.

By that point, I had already read both Sholem Aleichem's autobiography *From the Fair* (published in Yiddish in 1916, but not released in a full English translation until 1985), as well as *My Father, Sholom Aleichem* (the biography Marie Waife-Goldberg published about her famous father in 1968).

On page 231 of *From the Fair*, Sholem Aleichem talks about the day he met Elimelech Loyeff—his future father-in-law—for the first time.

> Listen here, young fellow, let me ask you something, old Loyev sang out. "My son [Joshua] tells me that you're just as knowledgeable in our holy Jewish books as in their secular ones. Do you remember what Rashi says about the daughters of Zelophehad?"
>
> Then commenced a long-winded discussion on Rashi. And Rashi led to the Talmud. At which followed a learned disquisition about scholarship and Haskala, as is usual among Jews who are at home in all the Commentaries.

I had read these words in Curt Leviant's translation from 1985, but they hadn't registered. Since I had no appreciation yet for the Daughters of Zelophehad, the significance of this reference to them in Sholem Aleichem's autobiography had gone right over my head... until the day Richard was in a Torah Study discussion of Parsha Pinchas!

So my question to you is this: How could a story that is so present in our Biblical literature have been disappeared for centuries? After all, this is a critical part of the narrative, at the end of the Book of Numbers, when the Israelites—after all their years of wandering in the desert—are finally going to enter the Land. This is not one of those weeks when the poor Bar/Bat Mitzvah student has to struggle through the rules of Kashrut or whatever. Parsha Pinchas is in a really critical part of the Torah, right before we begin the Book of Deuteronomy in which Moses gives his final exhortation and then the people cross over the Jordan.

And there, at this point of maximum promise and peril, we learn the story of the five daughters of a man named Zelophehad, and three times, we hear their names. Mahlah, No'ah, Hoglah, Milcah, and Tirzah go to the Tent of Meeting:

> They stood before Moses, Eleazar the priest,
> the chieftains, and the whole assembly, at the
> entrance of the Tent of Meeting, and they said,
> "Our father died in the wilderness. He was
> not one of the faction, Korah's faction, which
> banded together against the Lord, but died for
> his own sin; and he has left no sons. Let not
> our father's name be lost to his clan just because
> he had no son! Give us a holding among our
> father's kinsmen!"

> Moses brought their case before the Lord. And
> the Lord said to Moses, "The plea of Zelophe-
> had's daughters is just: you should give them a
> hereditary holding among their father's kinsmen;
> transfer their father's share to them."

> Further, speak to the Israelite people as follows:
> "If a man dies without leaving a son, you shall
> transfer his property to his daughter."

The five daughters of Zelophehad are in the Torah, and they are in Sholem Aleichem's autobiography, and therein lies our challenge with respect to selective memory: Our culture, like all cultures, prizes some pieces of our story above others, cherry-picks what it wants to remember, and disappears the rest. And yet, at least in our Jewish Tradition, the original texts are still there, waiting for us to find them, and pull stories back into significance. Defy Conventional Wisdom! Honor the text! Put the facts back into the legend!

What is happening in Sholem Aleichem's life, in his telling, when he reaches this part of his autobiography? Well, he's been wandering around as an itinerant teacher, and he is at an inn one night, and he meets a young man named Joshua Loyeff who is the son of a prominent local landowner (something very rare for Jews in the Russian Pale of Settlement in those days). After speaking with this teenager (really, Sholem Aleichem was a very young man at that time), Joshua Loyeff says: "You know, I think my father would really like you, so I'm going to tell him about you."

And Joshua went home and brought his father Elimelech Loyeff back to the inn to meet Solomon Rabinowitz (aka Sholem Aleichem), and the first thing that Elimelech Loyeff wants to know, according to Sholem Aleichem, is: Have you read Rashi's commentary on the Daughters of Zelophehad? And young Solomon Rabinowitz says: "Yes, in fact I have, sir." And they proceed to have a discussion, and Sholem Aleichem describes how a crowd gathered around them, and the crowd was riveted by his erudition.

What are we to make of this?

I used to say to myself: "Well… maybe?" Is this a true memory? Did Sholem Aleichem actually have this conversation with Elimelech Loyeff the first time they met, or is this just the memory of a man knowing he is close to death—a man who has been ill for a long time—is this just the memory of a man who at the time of his death is still plagued by the fact that he had four daughters and one ward, and had been personally responsible for five dowries? Did the story of the Daughters of Zelophehad resonate with Sholem Aleichem at the end of his life such that he put them into his story thinking he "remembered" them?

And then I read Rashi. Rashi was also a man blessed with daughters but no sons. Rashi had three daughters, and Rashi taught them Torah, and Rashi's daughters became the mothers of sons who became famous scholars in their own right, and helped to secure their grandfather's legacy. And Rashi's commentary about the Daughters of Zelophehad is quite long and very positive in tone.

So now, as I think about all of this again, I think maybe this is a true fact about the day Sholem Aleichem first met Elimelech Loyeff. Maybe Elimelech Loyeff asked young Solomon Rabinowitz (aka Sholem Aleichem) about the Daughters of Zelophehad because he wanted to know if this young man would be a good tutor for the children who currently resided at his estate in Sofievka? After all, Elimelech Loyeff knew something that Solomon Rabinowitz did not know: There were three girls in Sofievka awaiting Loyeff's return to the estate.

Let's assume that this is a true fact. Let's assume Elimelech Loyeff did ask Solomon Rabinowitz if he knew Rashi's commentary on the Daughters of Zelophehad? Why might he have asked this? Maybe what he was thinking was: Would this young man be an appropriate teacher for these three girls of mine—my daughter Olga (age 15) and my granddaughters Manya (age 9) and Natasha (age 5)—who are back in Sofievka?

If I bring Solomon Rabinowitz (aka Sholem Aleichem) back to Sofievka, will he be a good teacher? Or is he the kind of young man who will say: "Girls?!? No Way!!! I'm not going to waste my time teaching girls!!!"

So maybe the fact that Solomon Rabinowitz did know about Rashi's commentary on the Daughters of Zelophehad, which is, in fact, a very positive commentary about these five woman and their role in the Torah, maybe this was the reassurance that Elimelech Loyeff was looking for?

Of course, we are never going to know. We do not have Elimelech Loyeff here. We do not have Solomon Rabinowitz here. We do not have Ransom Stoddard here to interview about what really happened on the day that Liberty Valance died. But we do know that Parsha Pinchas and Parsha Mattot/Mas'ei roll around every summer, and maybe now, we will pay more attention to them?

© Janet Shafner (2006)

I want to close by bringing us back to Rabbi Carie's wonderful D'var Torah last Saturday before she left on vacation. Our subject last Saturday was the talking donkey, or, as this creature is best known, "Balaam's Ass." Maybe I knew before last Saturday that Balaam's Ass was in fact a female donkey, but if so, then that is another fact that I had also forgotten. So when I was listening to Rabbi Carie's D'var Torah last Saturday, I was extremely moved because, of course, Rabbi Carie made clear that this voice—the voice of Balaam's Ass—was a female voice.

A man named Balaam is beating "his" animal, and finally she turns to him and says: "Why are you beating me?" And Rabbi Carie asked us to imagine what Balaam's Ass was thinking at that moment. Then Rabbi Carie talked in her D'var Torah about domestic violence and that whole thread that was part of her D'var Torah last Shabbat. But what I was sitting here thinking was: Is this story of Balaam's Ass an introduction to the story of the Daughters of Zelophehad? Is this where the authors of our most revered text warn us about men who refuse to listen to female voices?

This female being—one of God's creatures—is being beaten without mercy! When Rabbi Carie asked us what we thought Balaam's Ass was thinking, we called out: Why don't you trust me? I've been your faithful companion all these years and I've never done anything like this before and suddenly I'm calling your attention to something, so why are you beating me instead of asking yourself "What is my faithful companion trying to tell me?" Is there something I see that you—Balaam—do not see? And that is, of course, when the angel reveals itself to Balaam.

My life's work has been about recovering the voices of women, always in dismay over how the voices of women are systematically disappeared from our culture. I am not going say anything about the political year—2016—that just ended. I'm going to leave that for you to think about later. But I do want to say this: Let us not allow the legend to become fact. Let us not cherry-pick from our most revered text, leaving out things that may be uncomfortable for us. Let us strive to see what is actually there in the text, and in this case, one of the things that is obviously there in the final three parshot of the Book of Numbers is the celebration of the female voice, and the affirmation by God to Moses and the Elders in the Tent of Meeting and the people of Israel that yes indeed these five Daughters of Zelophehad—Mahlah, No'ah, Hoglah, Milcah, and Tirzah—are essential members of the Jewish People and they each deserve a portion in the Land.

Shabbat Shalom!

**2018
Communications Contest**

Second Place

Jan Lisa Huttner

Speech

D'var Torah on Parsha Pinchas

Marianne Wolf-Astrauskas, NFPW President

Teri Ehresman, Contest Director

BRIEF NOTE ON NAMES

Just like in the case of C-H-A-N-U-K-A-H versus H-A-N-U-K-K-A-H, there are choices to be made. Is the English name of this great Yiddish author "Sholem Aleichem" or "Sholom Aleykhem"? Was his real name "Solomon Rabinowitz" or "Sholom Rabinovich"? Was his second daughter's name "Lyala" or "Lola" or "Lala"? In all cases, someone has before them a name that was originally written in either Cyrillic characters or in Hebrew characters, but in a world of search engines, where does one look for the "right" English translation? I have looked everywhere.

In general, for the sake of consistency, I have chosen whatever name was used by the creators of *Fiddler on the Roof* because these are the English names which are most familiar to us now. But when I am quoting someone else, I do not change the actual text of the quote. And so, for example, when I quoted from the Regina Mantell essay in the 1948 *Sholem Aleichem Panorama*, I kept the names the way she spelled them: "Madame Sholom Aleichem" and "Hodl."

In this, as in all cases, all the final editing decisions were made by me (especially with respect to punctuation).

ACKNOWLEDGMENTS

Counting from 2000 to 2018, I have seen almost three dozen live performances of *Fiddler on the Roof* on stages from West Palm Beach, Florida, to Regina, Saskatchewan. Since I lived in Chicago for most of this time, many of these performances were in Metro Chicago, from national touring companies who made stops at big theatres in the Chicago Loop, to local companies spread all across the region (from Lincolnshire in the northern suburbs, to Aurora in the western suburbs, to Munster in the southern suburbs). I also flew in from Chicago to see the 2004 Broadway revival. It was controversial… so I saw it twice before writing my review for the *World Jewish Digest*, and then I saw it a third time after major changes were made to the cast.

I have seen some very famous actors play Tevye onstage—including Theodore Bikel, Harvey Fierstein, Alfred Molina, and Chaim Topol—and I have seen some actors in supporting roles who were not well-known then but are fairly well known now (such as Erik Liberman, Sally Murphy, and Robert Petkoff). I know for sure that many of these actors were Jewish, but most of them probably were not.

I owe each and every one of these performers—the known and the novices—a huge debt of gratitude. Every single stage performance of *Fiddler on the Roof* has been a source of inspiration to me. No matter how many times I see it, I am never bored. It is always different. Seeing the actors stretch, as they step into the TRADITION of *Fiddler on the Roof,* is always thrilling. I have learned more from watching Anatevkans do their thing on stage than I have learned from all the books, articles, reviews, or interviews in my queue. And the same goes for the people working behind the scenes (directors, designers, choreographers, musicians); they all work tirelessly to make their own *Fiddler on the Roof* memorable and they always succeed.

Next I thank family members of the creators who gave me valuable insights and offered encouragement, particularly Marc Aronson (the son of Boris Aronson), Wendy Marcus Lebson (the granddaughter of Marie Waife-Goldberg and the great granddaughter of Sholem Aleichem), Bella Meyer (the granddaughter of Marc Chagall), and Harry Stein (the son of Joseph Stein). I also include Frank Rich in this category. He was Harry Stein's friend long before he was a theater critic for the *New York Times*, so he attended several performances of *Fiddler on the Roof* before the Broadway debut in 1964. Rich gave me lengthy, generous feedback on a very early draft way back in 2003, and he also connected me with the Aronson family so I could post examples of Aronson's set design on my blog.

Next I thank all of the people who have assisted me at the New York Public Library for the Performing Arts at Lincoln Center for over almost two decades now, including desk clerks, experts in Special Collections, and all of the security guards who make sure that these priceless documents remain intact. To produce this book, I owe special gratitude to photograph librarian Jeremy Megraw and to Thomas Lisanti in "Permissions." In this category, I also include Christopher Pennington (Executive Director of the Robbins Rights Trust and a Director and Treasurer of the Jerome Robbins Foundation), and all the people who agreed to permit use of the precious images to which they now own the copyright.

A hearty thanks to all of the editors who have published my work over the years, most especially Aaron Cohen, Cindy Sher and Stefanie Bregman (*JUF News*), Alana Newhouse (*Forward*), Martha Richards (WomenArts), and Simona Fuma Weinglass (*World Jewish Digest*). In this category, I also include all of the artists, authors, filmmakers, and musicians who graciously granted me time for an interview.

Next I thank all of the teachers who saw "something" in me and guided me forward. This list is incredibly long but here are some of the teachers, many of whom are long gone, who filled me with wonder: George Doskow, Leon Goldstein, Janellen Huttenlocher, Simon Kaplan, Amy Kass, Leon Kass, Theodore Mischel, Louis Paul, Jane Platt, Nathaniel Stampfer, Manley Thompson, and Stephen Toulmin. In this category, I also add people who have been true mentors—and not just "bosses"—including: Kim Benziger, Ben Escobar, Karen Geisler, Bruce Mahon, Christine Malcolm, Jacob Morowitz, Bart Neuman, Iris Sepe, and Dolores Williams.

Next I thank all of the people who have provided feedback on one or more of my many Metro Chicago presentations. This list is huge so for now, let's just say you know who you are. I also thank all of the people who have provided feedback on presentations given since my move to Brooklyn. This is a relatively short list but it is definitely growing. Many of the people in these two categories are fellow congregants with whom I have worshiped at KAM Isaiah Israel and Kol Ami (in Chicago), or at Temple Beth Emeth and Park Slope Jewish Center (in Brooklyn).

Many more are friends made through shared struggle in various progressive organizations over the years including (but not limited to): American Association of University Women, Chicago YIVO Society, Hadassah, Illinois Woman's Press Association, International Women Associates, and ORT. My father Eddie Huttner was a member of Painters District Council #10 of Great Essex County, New Jersey, and I was raised to be "a joiner."

Next I thank all of the people who have worked in various capacities to help me complete production on this book, including Sylvia Franklin, Kris Lockett and Lis Sowerbutts (production managers), plus Alma Garcia (research assistant), Brigid Presecky (editorial assistant), Dana Sinn (transcriptionist), Melissa Wilks and Allison Nordin (graphic artists), and Pilar Wyman (indexer). Huge thanks to my writing coaches Bonnie Kustner (2014 edition) and Katherine Factor (2018 edition).

My parents (Helene and Edwin Huttner) and my in-laws (Juanita and William Miller) are not gone. They live on—in my mind and in my heart—with every breath. In this category, I also include my grandmother, my mother's mother, Sophie Slotnick Hecht. When I ask myself about the source of my own "traditions," my thoughts dance merrily back to the sights and sounds and smells of her kitchen.

And finally a few words spoken directly to the two people, my husband Richard Bayard Miller and my BFF Dorthea Juul, who keep me grounded on Planet Earth: Your patience, your forbearance, your encouragement, and your love… without both of you… well, I do not know where I would be, but I would not be "here" today.

Sholem Aleichem Yahrzeit (circa 1955)

ABOUT MARIE WAIFE-GOLDBERG

Marie Waife-Goldberg—aka Maroussia Rabinowitz—was born in Odessa in 1892. She was the fourth daughter of Solomon and Olga Rabinowitz, and the fifth of their six children. Maroussia received her degree from the University of Lausanne in Switzerland before joining her parents in New York in 1914. She died in New York in 1985 at the age of 93. Maroussia Rabinowitz married Benjamin Waife in 1917. He became a well-known author, writing under the name B.Z. Goldberg. The Waifes had two sons (Sholem and Mitchell), and four grandchildren (Robert, Ronald, Sandra and Wendy). Benjamin Waife died in Tel Aviv in 1972.

According to their granddaughter Wendy Marcus Lebson, many Yahrzeit celebrations honoring Sholem Aleichem were held at her grandmother's New York apartment, and Marc Chagall participated on some occasions when he was in town. The annual Yahrzeit celebrations are now held at the Brotherhood Synagogue in Gramercy Park. My husband Richard and I attended in 2012 at Wendy's invitation. We also attended in 2013 and 2014. (Update 2018: We also attended in 2015, 2016, 2017, and 2018.)

ABOUT THE AUTHOR

Marie Waife-Goldberg was born in Odessa, where her father moved his family temporarily after losing a fortune in the market crash of 1892. She spent
her childhood in Kiev and her youth in Switzerland and Italy. In December
1914, after graduating from the University of Lausanne, she came with her
father and family to the United States.

At the commemoration of the twenty-fifth anniversary of her father's death,
she delivered a talk in New York City about his life, which brought invitations
to lecture in other cities and led to a lecture tour through the major countries
of Latin America.

Mrs. Waife-Goldberg was married in 1917 to Benjamin Waife, then a student,
who later became known as columnist and author B. Z. Goldberg. They have
two married sons and four grandchildren.

© Marie Waife-Goldberg (1968)

© Mayaan Haim-Rothbart (2017)

ABOUT JAN LISA HUTTNER

I am a graduate of St. John's College in Annapolis, Maryland ("the Great Books School"), and I hold masters degrees from Harvard University (Ed.M. Educational Psychology), the State University of New York at Binghamton (M.A. History and Philosophy of the Social and Behavioral Sciences), and the University of Chicago (M.A. Human Development). As a graduate student, I published my master's thesis "Egocentrism: A Defense of Pre-Reflexive Experience" in *International Studies in Philosophy*, and I gave three different presentations at annual meetings of the Jean Piaget Society. I received an affirmative action grant while at SUNY-Binghamton, and fellowships from the Thomas J. Watson Foundation and the G.D. Searle Foundation.

From 1984 to 2002, I worked as a healthcare computer consultant for two "Big Eight" accounting firms, Coopers and Lybrand (now PricewaterhouseCoopers) and Peat Marwick Mitchell (now KPMG), as well as Superior Consultant Company (a boutique healthcare firm). During those years, I carved out a niche for myself as a nationally recognized expert on behavioral health, home care, and long-term care, publishing regularly and making frequent appearances at professional conferences. I left consulting in 2002 to attend to family health issues.

I began writing professionally in 2003, quickly amassing local and national awards for my print pieces and online posts. I received three "Silver Feathers" for writer-of-the-year from the Illinois Woman's Press Association in 2005, 2006, and 2010. Several of my submissions were also sent up from IWPA to the National Federation of Press Women, where I won further recognition in 2005, 2010, and 2018 in their national contests.

In 2004, when I was Director of College and University Relations for AAUW-Illinois, I started the WITASWAN (**W**omen **in** **t**he **A**udience **S**upporting **W**omen **A**rtists **N**ow) project. In 2007, I began collaborating with Martha Richards of WomenArts—the Fund for Women Artists—to turn WITASWAN into an annual celebration called International SWAN Day.

In 2011, I published *Penny's Picks: 50 Movies by Women Filmmakers*, with introductory chapters on the history of WITAS-WAN® Events and International SWAN Day, as well as reviews of 50 films by women directors and/or screenwriters. The first International SWAN Day was held in 2008. Since that time, International SWAN Day has been celebrated at more than 1,500 separate events all around the world.

I relocated from Chicago to Brooklyn in September 2012 when my husband made a job change. This proved to be a happy occurrence that enabled me to spend unlimited time doing archival research (especially in the extensive collection of the Jerome Robbins Papers) once I lived just a train ride away from the New York Public Library for the Performing Arts at Lincoln Center.

All I had wanted way back in May 2000 was a relaxing vacation; I had no idea my life was about to take such a profound turn.

> Two roads diverged in a wood, and I—
> I took the one less traveled by,
> And that has made all the difference.
>
> – Robert Frost (1916)

© (1959)

BIBLIOGRAPHY

The purpose of the 2014 edition was to celebrate the first Broadway performance of *Fiddler on the Roof*, and the purpose of this 2018 edition is to celebrate the 100th birthday of Jerome Robbins, as well as whet the reader's appetite for more. What follows is a bibliography of some of the materials I have read since 2002. Included here are only the materials that pertain to this book.

Key Texts

Sholem Aleichem's eight Tevye stories
    1948 English translation by Frances Butwin
    1996 English translation by Hillel Halkin
    2009 English translation by Aliza Shevrin

Sholem Aleichem's Ethical Will (1915)
    Selected works of Sholem Aleykhem, edited by Marvin Zuckerman and Marion Herbst. Malibu, Calif: Joseph Simon/Pangloss Press, 1994.

From the Fair: The Autobiography of Sholom Aleichem, translated by Curt Leviant. New York: Viking Press,1985.

Fiddler on the Roof, published in arrangment with Crown Publishers, Inc. New York: Limelight Editions, 1964. Book by Joseph Stein, music by Jerry Bock, and lyrics by Sheldon Harnick.

First Impressions, adapted by Abe Burrows from Helen Jerome's dramatization of Austen's *Pride and Prejudice*. New York: Samuel French, 1959. Music and lyrics by Robert Goldman, Glenn Paxton, and George Weiss.

Book of Numbers (Jewish Publication Society's *JPS Tanakh*)
    Shabbat Pinchas: *Numbers* 25:10–30:1
    Shabbat Mattot/Mas'ei: *Numbers* 33:1–36:13

Selected Primary Sources

Austen, Jane. *Pride and Prejudice*, with an introduction by Anna Quindlen. New York: Modern Library, 2000.

Chagall, Bella. *Burning Lights*, translated by Norbert Guterman. New York: Schocken, 2013.

Chagall, Marc. *My Life*, translated by Elisabeth Abbott. Cambridge, MA: Da Capo Press, 1994.

Goldberg, Edwin and Janet Morder. *Mishkan HaNefesh: Machzor for the Days of Awe*. New York: CCAR Press, 2015.

Goldwin, Robert A. "St. John's College Asks John Locke Some Questions." *The College*. Annapolis, MD: St. John's College, April, 1971.

Grafstein, Melech W. *Sholom Aleichem Panorama* (especially the contributions of I.D. Berkowitz, Marie W. Goldberg, Lala Kaufman, and Regina Mantell). London, ON: Jewish Observer, 1948.

Nussbaum, Emily. "Horsey Set: The Upscale Temptations of 'Luck' and 'Downton Abbey.'" *The New Yorker*, January 23, 2012.

Perl, Arnold. *Tevya and His Daughters*. New York: Dramatists Play Service, Inc., 1958.

Waife-Goldberg, Marie. *My Father, Sholom Aleichem*. New York: Simon & Schuster Books, 1968.

Selected Secondary Sources

With all due respect to the authors of the secondary sources listed below, I learned a great deal from these sources about the "who what when where," but rarely did they address the "why." Therefore, the main benefit of all their hard work for me was to keep me digging ever deeper for answers to my own specific questions.

Altman, Richard and Mervin Kaufman. *The Making of a Musical: Fiddler on the Roof.* New York: Crown Publishers, 1971.

Dauber, Jeremy. *The Worlds of Sholem Aleichem: The Remarkable Life and Afterlife of the Man Who Created Tevye.* New York: Schocken Books, 2013.

Isenberg, Barbara. *Tradition: The Highly Improbable, Ultimately Triumphant Broadway-to-Hollywood Story of* Fiddler on the Roof, *the World's Most Beloved Musical.* New York: St. Martin's Press, 2014.

Kruckman, Herbert. *Our Sholem Aleichem.* New York, Kinderbuch Publictions, 1946.

Solomon, Alisa. *Wonder of Wonders: A Cultural History of* Fiddler on the Roof. New York: Metropolitan Books, 2013.

Additional Relevant Secondary Sources

Dabundo, Laura. *The Marriage of Faith: Christianity in Jane Austen and William Wordsworth.* Macon, GA: Mercer University Press, 2012.

Hillman, Jessica. *Echoes of the Holocaust on the American Musical Stage.* Jefferson, NC: McFarland, 2012.

Johnson, Claudia L. *Jane Austen's Cults and Cultures.* Chicago: University of Chicago Press. 2012.

Kagan, Andrew. *Marc Chagall.* New York: Abbeville Press, 1989.

Meyer, Franz. *Marc Chagall.* New York: Harry N. Abrams, 1964.

Ray, Joan Elizabeth Klingel. *Jane Austen for Dummies.* For Dummies Press, 2006.

Rich, Frank and Lisa Aronson. *The Theatre Art of Boris Aronson.* New York: Alfred A. Knopf, 1987.

Rodi, Robert. *Bitch in a Bonnet: Reclaiming Jane Austen from the Stiffs, the Snobs, the Simps and the Saps.* Create Space, 2011.

Wolf, Stacy. *Changed for Good: A Feminist History of the Broadway Musical.* Oxford: Oxford University Press, 2011.

Yaffe, Deborah. *Among the Janeites: A Journey through the World of Jane Austen Fandom.* New York: Mariner Books, 2013.

ADDITIONAL HUTTNER MATERIALS

"Everybody's *Fiddler*: A Researcher Finds a Link Long Denied Between Chagall and Sholom Aleichem." September 5, 2003. *Jewish Daily Forward.*

"From Halsted Street to Broadway: Jan Chats with Chicago Actress Sally Murphy." April 1, 2004. FF2Media.com/second citytzivi/.

"In the Eye of the Beholder: New Revivals of *Fiddler on the Roof* open in Chicago and New York." July 1, 2004. *World Jewish Digest.com.*

"Who was Boris Aronson?" July 12, 2004. FF2Media.com/secondcitytzivi/.

"Schwartz's *Tevye* Receives the Royal Treatment from NCJF." December 1, 2004. *World Jewish Digest* (distributed internationally by the Jewish Telegraphic Agency).

"Interview with Nir Bergman." March 12, 2004. FF2Media.com/secondcitytzivi/.

"Interview with Deborah Kampmeier." March 11, 2005. http://www.films42.com/chats/deborah_kampmeier.asp.

"Tevye's Family Adjusts to Life in America." August 1, 2006. *All About Jewish Theatre,* alljewishtheatre.org.

"Jonathan Wilson's 'Jewish Encounter' with Marc Chagall." March 1, 2007. FF2.Media.com/secondcitytzivi/.

"Munster's *Fiddler*." April 1, 2007. FF2media.com /second citytzivi/.

"Sholem Aleichem's *Stempenyu* Newly Reissued and Available in Paperback!" December 20, 2008. FF2Media.com/second citytzivi/.

"Jan Chats with Klezmer Musician Steve Greenman about *Stempenyu's Dream*." February 15, 2009. FF2Media.com/second citytzivi/.

"Chaim Topol's Farewell Tour." June 10, 2009. FF2Media.com/
    secondcitytzivi/.

Fiddler: Stage versus Screen." November 11, 2011. https://www.
    juf.org/news/blog.aspx?id=413176&blogid=13573.

"*Shylock and His Daughter* Opens in Oak Brook Tonight." July
    26, 2012. https://www.juf.org/news/arts.aspx?id=416229.

"Anatevka is Alive and Well on the Fox River." March 20, 2013.
    JUF News, (FF2Media.com/secondcitytzivi/).

"Jerome Robbins, Jewison and *Fiddler on the Roof.*" August 2,
    2013. *JUF News,* (FF2Media.com/secondcitytzivi/).

"Alisa Solomon brings 'Wonder of Wonders' to Chicago Area
    Nov. 22." November 20, 2013. *JUF News,* (FF2Media.com/
    secondcitytzivi/).

PHOTO CREDITS & PERMISSIONS

i. Front cover of *My Father, Sholom Aleichem* by Marie Waife-Goldberg. Copyright © Marie Waife-Goldberg (1968). Reprinted with the permission of Simon & Schuster Books, Inc. All Rights Reserved.

viii. Women's History Month lecture honoring Marie Waife-Goldberg. Congregation KAM Isaiah Israel, Chicago, IL. © Richard Bayard Miller (3/11/12).

11. The Daughters of Zelophehad, Numbers 27:1-11, illustration from *The Bible and Its Story: Taught by One Thousand Picture Lessons*, Volume 2, edited by Charles Francis Horne and Julius Brewer, 1908. Image 11-41. Permission granted from Forgotten Books (5/30/18). All Rights Reserved.

14. Taken in front of Moishe's Bake Shop on Second Avenue. © Sally Heckel (4/4/08).

17. Marc Chagall, *Green Violinist*. © Artists Rights Society (ARS), New York/ADAGP, Paris. Permission granted 2018. All Rights Reserved. https://guggenheim.org/artwork/802.

22. The grand chandelier in the City Cinemas Village East is in the shape of a Star of David. © Jan Lisa Huttner (7/31/13).

23. Maurice Schwartz's Yiddish Art Theatre on Second Avenue is now a Manhattan multiplex called the City Cinemas Village East. *Fiddler on the Roof* was the "Musical Monday" screening on October 15, 2018. © Jan Lisa Huttner (10/12/18).

24. *The Five Daughters of Zelophehad.* © Judith Klausner (2010). Used with written permission from the artist. All Rights Reserved.

26. "Tevya, Golda, their 7 Daughters and the Cow." © Manuel Bennett (1992). Used with written permission from the artist. All Rights Reserved.

28. *Tevye*, USA, 1939. Yiddish with English subtitles. Directed by Maurice Schwartz. © The National Center for Jewish Film. jewish-film.org/Catalogue/films/tevye.html .

30. Theatre at the Center cast members from left: Amy Olsen (Tzeitel), Audrey Billings (Hodel), Alyssa Trasher (Chava), Jessica Fisher (Shprintze), Kailey Snider (Bielke), and Lee Pelty (Tevye). "This is Mine" scene from Act One of *Fiddler on the Roof.* Courtesy of Bill Pullinsi (Artistic Director) & Richard Friedman (General Manager). © Greg Kolack (2007). All Rights Reserved.

32. Minskoff Theatre cast members from the left: Betsy Hogg (Bielke), Sally Murphy (Tzeitel), Alison Wallah (Shprintze), Harvey Fierstein (Tevye), Laura Shoop (Hodel), and Tricia Paoluccio (Chava). © Carol Rosegg (2005). All Rights Reserved.

34. Promotional shot for *Pride and Prejudice*. Cast from left: Julia Sawalha (Lydia), Jennifer Ehle (Elizabeth), Susannah Harker (Jane), Lucy Briers (Mary), and Polly Maberly (Kitty), plus Alison Steadman (Mrs. Bennet) and Benjamin Whitrow (Mr. Bennet). © BBC (1995). All Rights Reserved.

39. *First lmpressions* Original Broadway Cast album cover (1959). © Sony Music Entertainment. All Rights Reserved.

41. *First Impressions* (1959): Lizzie Bennet (Polly Bergen) is offered consolation by her sisters Jane (Phyllis Newman) and Kitty (Lauri Peters). © Friedman-Abeles. Billy Rose Theatre Division, The New York Public Library for the Performing Arts. All Rights Reserved.

42. *Daughters of Zelophehad*. © Iris Wexler (1985). Oil paint on stretched canvas. Used with written permission from the artist. All Rights Reserved.

46. Family photo of Solomon Rabinowitz (aka Sholem Aleichem) with his wife Olga and their first three children—Ernestina, Lyala, and Emma—circa 1890. From the archives of the YIVO Institute for Jewish Research, New York. All Rights Reserved.

49. Loyeff Family Tree based on information gleaned from *My Father, Sholom Aleichem* by Marie Waife-Goldberg. © Jan Lisa Huttner (2018). All Rights Reserved.

51. Rabinowitz Family Tree based on information gleaned from *My Father, Sholom Aleichem* by Marie Waife-Goldberg. © Jan Lisa Huttner (2018). All Rights Reserved.

52. A skeptical Hodel observes as Perchik teaches her younger sisters a lesson from the Bible. Permission granted by Oceanside High School (NY) on 3/6/17. All Rights Reserved.

54. *Downton Abbey* 2010 (cast from left): Laura Carmichael (Lady Edith), Michelle Dockery (Lady Mary), and Jessica Brown Findlay (Lady Sybil). Courtesy of Carnival Film & Television Limited/Masterpiece. All Rights Reserved.

57. Tea with the "Ladies." © Rob Copeland Photography (9/15/18). All Rights Reserved.

58. "Sabbath Prayer" scene from *Fiddler on the Roof*. Original 1964 cast members from left: Zero Mostel (Tevye), Maria Karnilova (Golde), Joanna Merlin (Tzeitel), Julia Migenes (Hodel), Tanya Everett (Chava), Marilyn Rogers (Shprintze), and Linda Ross (Bielke). © Eileen Darby Images, Inc. (1964). All Rights Reserved.

63. Celebrating the 100th birthday of Jerome Robbins, based on cover art for the original Broadway production of *Fiddler on the Roof* in 1964. © Jan Lisa Huttner & Sharon Rosenzweig (2018).

70. "The Daughters of Zelophehad" from *The Bible and its Story Taught in One Thousand Picture Lessons*. Edited by Charles F. Horne and Julius A. Brewer (1908). Source: WikiCommons: http://en.wikipedia.org/wiki/Daughters_of_Zelophehad. Forgotten Books has waived rights to this image.

81. *The Daughters of Zelophehad*. Three 48" x 84" panels, oil on canvas. © Janet Shafner (2006). Used with written permission from the artist's estate. All Rights Reserved.

83. National Federation of Women's Press Mission Statement: "*To promote professionalism and ethical activities in journalism and communications by providing valuable networking, peer recognition* and *mentoring opportunities. To continually work to protect the rights of a* free *press within the First Amendment of the US Constitution.*" https://nfpw.org/.

88. Benjamin and Marie Waife-Goldberg with Marc Chagall circa 1955. Family photo courtesy of granddaughter Wendy Marcus Lebson.

89. Back cover of *My Father, Sholom Aleichem* by Marie Waife-Goldberg. © Marie Waife-Goldberg (1968). Reprinted with the permission of Simon & Schuster Books, Inc. All Rights Reserved.

90. Jan Lisa Huttner as "Madame Sholem Aleichem" at City Cinemas Village East, formerly Maurice Schwartz's Yiddish Art Theatre. © Mayaan Haim-Rothbart (Konfetti Studios 2017).

93. Eddie Huttner and his two daughters—Roberta (left) and Jan (right)—celebrate his parents' 50th wedding anniversary. Newark, New Jersey (1959).

110. Gravesite of Solomon and Olga Rabinowitz. Mount Carmel Cemetery, Queens, New York. © Alan Zarrow (2016).

INDEX

WHAT DID YOU THINK OF
TEVYE'S DAUGHTERS:
NO LAUGHING MATTER ?

Thank you for purchasing this book. It is a labor of love representing almost two decades of research. I know you could have picked any number of books to read, but you picked my "appetizer," and for that I am extremely grateful. I hope that it adds value to your love for *Fiddler on the Roof*.

This is a unique book by an independent author. Therefore your feedback is critical. I would be so grateful if you would post a comment about it on Facebook or Twitter, or post a review on Amazon or Goodreads.

FOLLOW THIS LINK TO LEAVE A REVIEW:

HTTPS://WWW.AMAZON.COM/JAN-LISA-HUTTNER/E/B007102L1I

© Alan Zarrow (2016)

Made in United States
North Haven, CT
12 February 2022

16049056R00074